Time and the Valley

The Past, Present and Future of the Upper Ogwen Valley

David Hubback

GWASG CARREG GWALCH

To my grandchildren
May they enjoy the Nant Ffrancon
as much as I have.

Front Cover:
Llyn Bochlwyd and Nant Ffrancon
from an original painting by David Woodford.

Back Cover:
Climbing the Direct Route on Glyder Fach.
Photo by Steve Ashton.

Coloured illustrations from original painting:—

Facing Page 32:
Ogwen and Tryfan by David Woodford.

Facing Page 48
Cwm Coch, Nant Ffrancon.
Screenprint by John Piper.

Facing Page 64:
Ogwen and Tryfan from Foel Goch
by David Woodford.

Facing Page 80
Snowdon from Glyder Fach
by David Woodford.

ISBN: 0 86381 039 X

First published 1987 by Gwasg Carreg Gwalch
Capel Garmon, Llanrwst, Gwynedd,
Wales.
Tel: 06902 261

CONTENTS

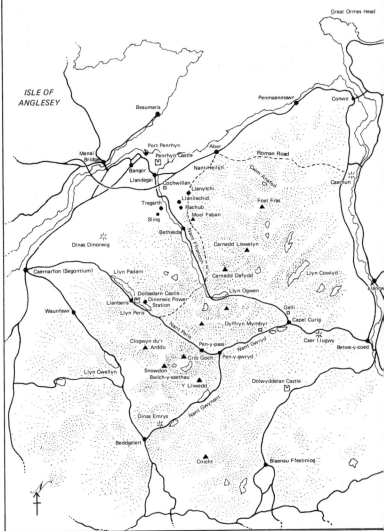

MAP OF PART OF
GWYNEDD, NORTH WALES.

SCALE

Kilometres

Miles

ISLE OF ANGLESEY

Great Ormes Head

Penmaenmawr

Conwy

Beaumaris

Port Penrhyn

Aber

Roman Road

Menai Bridge

Penrhyn Castle

Nant-Heilyn

Cwm Anafon

Caerhun

Bangor

Cochwillan

Llandegai

Llanylchi

Tregarth

Llanllechid

Foel Fras

Rachub

Sling

Moel Faban

Bethesda

Dinas Dinorwig

Carnedd Llewelyn

Nant Ffrancon

Carnedd Dafydd

Llyn Cowlyd

Caernarfon (Segontium)

Llyn Padarn

Llyn Ogwen

Llanrwst

Dolbadarn Castle

Dinorwic Power Station

Gelli

Llanberis

Llyn Peris

Capel Curig

Waunfawr

Nant Peris

Dyffryn Mymbyr

Caer Llugwy

Pen-y-pass

Nant Gwryd

Betws-y-coed

Clogwyn du'r Arddu

Crib Goch

Pen-y-gwryd

Snowdon

Bwlch-y-saethau

Dolwyddelan Castle

Llyn Cwellyn

Y Lliwedd

Nant Gwynant

Dinas Emrys

Beddgelert

Cnicht

Blaenau Ffestiniog

N

Maps: Jeremy Yates

FOREWORD

This book is about the past, present and possible future of one of the most beautiful and dramatic valleys in the high mountains of North Wales. The book concentrates on a stretch of mountainous country, about 7 miles long and 3 miles wide, through which the Ogwen river flows from where it rises above Llyn Ogwen to where it leaves the Nant Ffrancon at the slate quarrying town of Bethesda. Although I am concerned mainly with only twenty-five square miles of country, my other dimension is time from the last Ice Age until the present.

When I started writing this book I knew the valleys and mountains well but not their past, nor many of the forces working on their inhabitants at present. In finding out I have received much help from Gwenno Caffell of the Llandegai and Llanllechid Archaeological Society, Frances Lynch of the University College of North Wales, Tomas Roberts, the assistant archivist at the College, Esme Kirby of the Snowdonia National Park Society and David Woodfood of the Friends of the Dyffryn Ogwen and whose striking pictures embellish this book. I have been greatly helped too by Simon Lappington, the National Trust Head Warden on the Carneddau Estate, Ellis Williams, one time Warden of Idwal Nature Reserve, and by many others in and around the Nant Ffrancon.

I am much indebted to John Piper and to Kelpra Editions for permitting me to include his superb screenprint of Cwm Coch, to Jeremy Yates for drawing the maps, and to Daphne Bonner for her first rate typing of my manuscript, Welsh place names notwithstanding.

Above all I owe a great deal to Mr and Mrs Williams and their son William of Maes Caradoc Farm for patiently answering my innumerable questions about sheep farming and the Nant Ffrancon.

November 1986   David Hubback

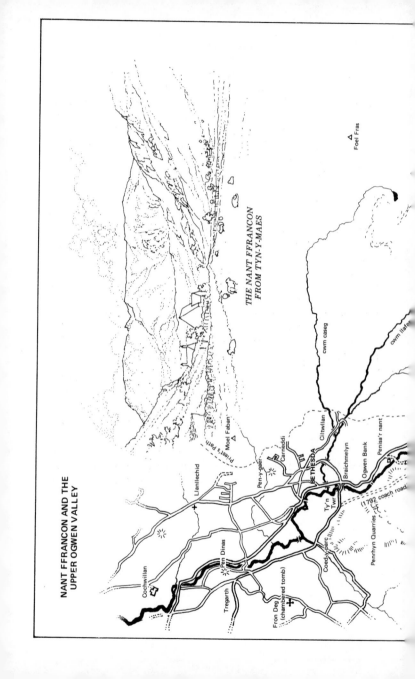

NANT FFRANCON AND THE
UPPER OGWEN VALLEY

THE NANT FFRANCON
FROM TYN-Y-MAES

Foel Fras

cwm caseg

cwm llafar

Cochwillan

Llanllechid

Pen-y-gaer

Priest's Path

Moel Faban

Carneddi

Pen Dinas

Tregarth

BETHESDA

Ty'n
Twr

Ciltwllan

Braichmelyn

Ogwen Bank

Penisa'r nant

Fron Deg
(chambered tomb)

Coed-y-parc

Penrhyn Quarries

(1792 coach road)

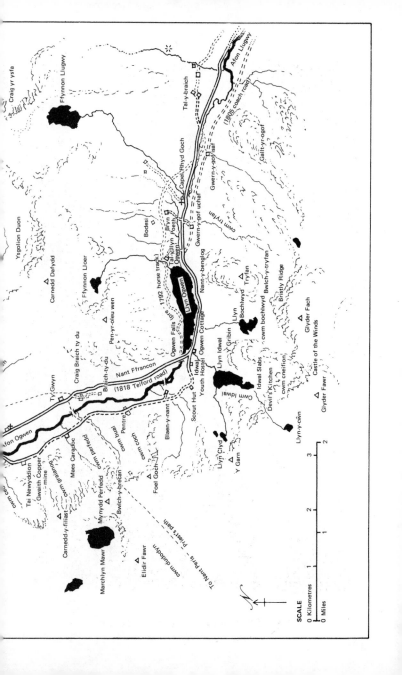

Nant Ffrancon from above Dolawen
(etching by David Woodford)

CHAPTER 1

Maes Caradoc and Nant Ffrancon

I was nine years old when I first saw Nant Ffrancon. I and my sisters had been taken over by my mother to visit some cousins at Maes Caradoc, a sheep farm on the old road halfway down the valley between Llyn Ogwen and the quarrying village of Bethesda. My cousins were staying in a cottage which my father, a keen rock climber and walker, had found in 1909 and had, without any hesitation, rented from the Penrhyn Estate for ten shillings a year. The cottage had at that time been empty for some time and its slate roof needed repair, the previous tenants having been two quarrymen's families who had moved out after the end of the long strike and lockout at the Penrhyn Quarry from 1900 − 1903. At the end of the strike the proprietor, Lord Penrhyn, had refused to employ many of the quarrymen especially if they had been active in the quarrymen's union. Those who had lived at Maes Caradoc were just two families out of a total of about 1,000 who had had to leave the quarry and seek work elsewhere, either in other local quarries or in the coalmines in South Wales, or even emigrating to North America and Patagonia.

Although the roof was in bad condition, the cottage walls were built of slate rock 2½ feet thick and the timbers were still sound. It was easy to convert the two cottages into one by cutting a door through the party wall. The cottages had been built early in the 19th century in the traditional croglofft style of the front door opening straight into a high living room with two little low bedrooms, the upper one of which was reached by a steep stair from the living room onto a small gallery. The living room had a big iron kitchen range surrounded with large slate slabs on which concentric circles were carved. One window looked down the valley to the quarry tips in the distance, the other across sheep pens up the valley to the Glyderau which are often obscured by cloud. There was also a back kitchen, added about 1890, lit by a skylight and a window over the sink looking up a steep little rocky field where sheep and lambs grazed before being sorted in the pens built against the back of the cottage. Beyond was the rocky bed of a swiftly flowing stream

Maes Caradoc Farm and Nant Ffrancon
(woodcut by Ruth Vale)

draining Cwm Perfedd a thousand feet further up the mountain.
My father had the roof repaired, but otherwise kept the cottages
in their original state, being entirely content with the simplest of
furniture. He would sometimes walk the sixty miles from Chester
near where he was living, and, if the weather was fine, sleep out
on Heather Terrace halfway up Tryfan before dropping down to
Maes Caradoc early in the morning. He brought his Cambridge

Maes Caradoc Cottage and sheep pens.

friends there and taught them rock climbing, even the totally unathletic girl to whom he got engaged at Maes Caradoc and who was to become my mother. Both my parents got enormous pleasure from Maes Caradoc in spite of frequent rainy days. But my father was killed on the Western Front in 1917 and the cottage was, for the next fifteen years, run by one of his sisters.

I do not remember being struck on my first visit by the fact that cooking was mainly on primus stoves, lighting was by oil lamps and candles and that water had to be fetched in buckets from the stream. I do, however, remember being much impressed by seeing my two cousins, aged about 17 and 20, arriving back in triumph from some new climb they had done above the Idwal Slabs at the head of the valley with coils of climbing rope slung across their shoulders and wearing tough tweed jackets and climbing breeches. They seemed to me imbued with all the glamour of mountaineering. While I doubted whether I could ever do what they did, I had always liked mountain walking and cliff climbing and here in Nant Ffrancon was all I could wish for. It must have been then I fell in love with the valley.

Apart from an occasional day's visit, I did not go back to Maes Caradoc for any length of time until 1932, when my aunt gave up the cottage as her rock climbing son was going to work in Assam, and my mother, who had a passion for mountains and sea, took over again. She had water piped into the kitchen sink by means of a pipe thrust into the stream that came down the mountain behind the cottage. But otherwise life there remained simple. There was no question of a hot water system, let alone a bathroom and the Elsan lavatory was outside in a little extension to the main cottage, tactfully labelled Ty bach. We got our food by bicycling the three miles to Bethesda, the first half of which was on the rutted old road, before joining the main road Telford had built in 1818 down the other side of the valley.

Maes Caradoc farm, of which the cottage was an integral part, as its back wall formed one side of the sheep pen, was run simply too. John Jones, the farmer, a man with a beautiful voice and great skill in managing his sheep, ran his eight hundred acre farm with his wife and the help of a welsh cob. Most of the land on the flat valley floor leading down to the Ogwen River was marshy, but there was some grazing for the ten Welsh Black cattle normally kept and the eight hundred or so sheep, when they were not up on the mountain slopes. There was only one field where it was worthwhile cutting the grass for hay, though in the frequent wet summers the hay was of poor quality because of the great difficulty of drying. But, even without the present subsidies, the Jones seemed to make a reasonable though simple living, thanks to having their own milk, butter, eggs and a few vegetables. It was hard work looking after the sheep, though they had the help of neighbouring farmers when gathering the sheep for lambing, dipping and shearing, which at that time was entirely by hand. With the sheep grazing on the open mountains sheep farming had to be a communal activity; so the Jones' equally went to help their neighbours throughout the valley and sometimes further afield.

The farmland went up and over a 2,600 foot mountain Mynedd Perfedd, down to Marchlyn Mawr on the other side. The land included a large hanging valley or cwm, Cwm Perfedd, much of it boggy. It always seemed to me to act as a great sponge which kept the stream, which gave us our water supply, going even in the driest weather. In the cwm were the ruins of a small summer cottage or voty, which had been used in previous centuries as a shelter for whoever was looking after the sheep and goats in the summer. In earlier times goat milk and even sheep milk was made into cheese. Cwm Perfedd led up to a pass, Bwlch y Brecan, which at 2,200 feet provided a way through to the Llanberis Valley and Snowdon. At one time, a packhorse track used this short cut from Nant Ffrancon to Nant Peris.

Aerial photograph of Maes Caradoc Farm below
Cwm Perfedd and Elidir Fawr. Carnedd y Filiast
and Cwm Graianog on the right.
(Cambridge University Collection – copyright reserved)

CHAPTER 2

Nant Ffrancon and Nant y Benglog

Anyone who has not consulted the map and who enters Nant Ffrancon for the first time on the road from Bethesda and the North, must wonder whether it is a dead end or whether there is a way through. The flat valley floor two and a half miles long and half a mile wide, down which the Ogwen River meanders, is set off by steep rocky mountain slopes on both sides, running up to 3,000 feet, To the south, a rock barrier several hundred feet high, down which the Ogwen Falls tumble, seem to block any further progress especially as behind the rock barrier precipitous high mountains, the Glyderau, rise running at right angles across the line of the valley and seeming to shut it off completely. So Nant Ffrancon, with the huge quarry tips at one end and the high mountains forming its other three sides, seems in some sense a haven cut off from the world but for the main road running on the east side of the valley and the small farm road running on the west. The sense of peaceful seclusion is enhanced by the farm buildings strung at wide intervals along both roads, the few Welsh Black cattle in the meadows where they emerge from the marshland, and the flocks of sheep grazing right from the valley floor up to the mountain skyline.

The sense of peace is at its strongest at both ends of the valley. At Ceunant, the lower end, a rocky ridge, left smooth by the last glacier and covered with pine trees, separates a secluded little valley, fringed with old oaks and leading down to the large walled meadow of Dolawen farm, from the Ogwen river which, below the old bridge carrying the farm road to Tyn-y-maes, cuts through rock in a gorge overhung by more oaks. Both the small valley and the stretch of river now running swiftly, after meandering down the flat Nant Ffrancon, have their own magic together with a splendid view of Foel Goch, a sharp peak above Maes Caradoc, looking far higher than its 2,600 feet. About 100 yards down the river from the bridge is a large pool ideal for swimming in warm weather or for observing the dippers fishing. With the passage of time the turf on the bank has become perfect in colour and texture. There is a place for a camp fire on which to cook trout caught in the river.

At the upper end of Nant Ffrancon above Blaen-y-nant farmhouse the magic is alpine. Bright green meadows, criss-crossed by the fast flowing streams of a delta formed by the Ogwen river below the falls, run up to a cirque of rocks and the steep grass slopes rising by stages, first to the old road, and then to the ridge that hides Cwm Idwal.

It is only when the traveller follows either of the roads, which both climb the rock step, that he realises that the valley turns sharply to the east at Llyn Ogwen where the sharp rocky peak of Tryfan and the great bulk of the Carneddau mountains flank the pass towards Capel Curig. It is above the rock step that Nant Ffrancon ends and Nant-y-Benglog (*the valley of the skull)* begins, continuing beyond Llyn Ogwen to the watershed at an altitude of 1,000 feet on the road down to Capel Curig. Taken together, these valleys form an L-shaped pass through the high mountains. This book is concerned with these two valleys, including the stretch down the Penrhyn Quarry and the little town of Bethesda (which grew with the quarry) and the high surrounding mountains. In all, this is an area of about twenty-five square miles, the whole of which constitues the Upper Ogwen Valley.

There is a great contrast between the two sides of Nant Ffrancon. On the east side, Pen yr Oleu Wen rises sharply to a series of rocky crags and stony gulleys which turn purple in the light of the setting sun. There are no regular streams on this stony slope, only torrents in wet weather which sometimes bring down boulders onto the A5 road below. Further down Nant Ffrancon there are steep grassy slopes now increasingly covered with bracken and scrub. Here the only permanent stream is Afon Berthen which drains the bog above the ridge above Tyn-y-maes – a one time quarrymen's village at the lower end of the valley, now only a few houses, some farm buildings, two disused chapels and a motel. There are two other farms on the road between Tyn-y-maes and Ogwen – Ty Gwyn, a prosperous looking place set among trees, and the very much poorer looking Braich-ty-du, which has only a scatter of meadows along the valley bottom and hardly any grazing land on the mountain above, which is mainly rock and scree slopes.

The west side of the valley is just as striking, being made up of rock bastions surmounted by peaks like flying buttresses topped with pinnacles, forming a fine progression along the ridge. Between the rocky bastions there are hanging valleys, the cwms,

which were scooped out by tributary glaciers during the Ice Age and look like a series of comfortable armchairs leading down to a much sharper descent for the last 1,000 feet to the valley floor. Above Maes Caradoc there are boulders left perched on the slopes by the retreating ice, and the drama is enhanced by the different type of rock which make up the precipices below the peaks. Some are craggy, others slabbed. One, Carnedd y Filiast, marked with gentle undulations looks as if at one time the sea has been at work and, indeed, these slabs are fragments of an ancient sea beach preserved intact with the ripple marks on the sand.

The 3,000 foot high Glyder mountains, which close the southern end of the valley, are a different type again, being for the most part flat on top but with great precipices plunging down into Cwm Idwal and Cwm Bochlwyd, divided by the Gribin Ridge which provides a short cut to the summits. It is only as one walks up the valley that a pass 2,200 feet up appears between Bristly Ridge on Glyder Fach and the rocky peak of Tryfan.

On the west side of Nant Ffrancon there are four farms strung out along the old road, but only two of these are occupied by farming families. Indeed, out of the seven farmhouses in the valley only three are occupied by farmers. The other farmhouses are used by retired people, mountaineering clubs or students from Bangor University. There are no more farmhouses to be seen before the east end of Llyn Ogwen. From there up to the watershed at the top of Nant-y-Benglog (from where the River Ogwen flows west and the River Llugwy flows east down to Capel Curig and the Conwy Valley), there are three more farms, two of which are occupied by farming families. These farms are at an altitude of nearly 1000 feet and are therefore even more exposed to the elements than those down in Nant Ffrancon at about 650 feet. But somehow quite often the sun seems to shine in Nant-y-Benglog when the clouds remain stuck in Nant Ffrancon.

There is no farmhouse at the west end of Llyn Ogwen, but much activity from holiday-makers and climbers who started staying at Ogwen Cottage a century ago. Now there is a mountain

The view from Foel Goch looking east to Llyn Ogwen,
Nant-y-Benglog and Capel Curig. The Glyderau and Tryfan
are on the right, Pen yr Oleu Wen on the left.
(Photo by Steve Ashton)

training school there and an enlarged superbly equipped Idwal Youth Hostel and many people coming and going on the main mountain walks.

FLOWERS

In spite of the many walkers and the sheep, both flowers and birds do well in the valley. On the valley floor bog myrtle grows well, but so too, where the sheep are kept off the meadow, do the ordinary meadow flowers, including some orchids. Yellow welsh poppies are to be found, particularly round buildings. On the lower slopes foxgloves, and in season, bluebells abound. So too do the tiny yellow tormentil, the blue milkwort and the white heath bedstraw, which enliven the slopes making the hard work of climbing them so much more pleasurable. In boggy patches there is plenty of bog asphodel, water lobelia, cotton grass and sphagnum moss. More exciting are the pale pink spotted orchids and the yellow bog St. John's Wort. Along the rocky streams there is a wonderful series of saxifrages as the year goes on, starting with the purple saxifrage when snow is still lying and going on to the golden saxifrage and starry saxifrage. The ferns too and club mosses in the streams are of particular beauty.

The saxifrages are, of course, true alpine plants, as, indeed, are other plants found high up, particularly above Cwm Idwal. The most famous of these alpines is the snowdon lily *(lloydia serotina)* which is found near the Devil's Kitchen. Almost as rare is the dryas, a member of the rose family, which is found in two places in or near Nant Ffrancon — the dryas octopetala. Then there is the yellow globe flower, which from a distance looks rather like welsh poppies but can be seen in almost as fine a splendour as in the Alps. On the rocky slopes and right up on the summit ridges are a large variety of lichens which paint the boulders yellow, red and green in a most beautiful way.

BIRDS

The valley, though high, inhospitable and often stormy, attracts many birds. 180 species have been recorded along the whole length of the Ogwen river down to the sea. In the spring, wheatears, pied-wagtails, stone chats and rock pipits compete for the best perches on the walls and boulders of the lower farmland. Larks abound. Dippers, grey wagtails and sandpipers fish in the

Ogwen river and in the faster streams on the mountain slopes. There is usually at least one heron in the valley and several pair of mallard. Occasionally a pair of merganiser spend a few days on one of the pools on the Ogwen. There are plenty of crows and seagulls. The blackheaded gull breeds on some of the high mountain lakes and the herring gull comes for the tourists' leftover sandwiches.

Higher up, usually above 2,000 feet, there are ring ouzels among the rocks, and ravens and buzzards flying around the summit rocks. After being very scarce, peregrines are now coming back, thanks to the prohibition of harmful pesticides and the good work of the Idwal Nature Conservancy warden. On rare occasions a golden eagle visits the Carneddau mountains. Wrens can be found in the rocks, both low down and high up on the mountains, and occasionally at Easter there are snow bunting to be seen on the mountain tops, curiously unafraid of walkers and birdwatchers.

THE MOUNTAIN RIDGES

My father's description of the valley, in a letter of 1911, is as true today as then.

"This is a lovely place — a great wide mountain valley with a dark river running down between grassy or rocky banks; farther on there are pines and oak woods where the river jumps away over rocks dazzling white with foam. But up here it goes smoothly among the meadows which are blowing in the wind blue and golden with harebells and dandelions. Just now the river has flooded after the rains and great pools spread out into the fields and shine heavenly blue when the sky is clear. At the upper end of the valley the river comes down from Ogwen Lake rushing over tremendous falls which you can see from here as a thin white streak on the rocks. All round sun scorched the mountains stand, grass ridges or heathery, or great crags split by millions of frosts with their bases deep in the fragments which the rain and the wind bring down from them.

"That is where one climbs up gullies sounding with water streams or on rocky headlands grey and sun-warm at this time of the year, but icy cold in winter. When one gets on the top of them one sees right out to sea beyond Anglesey and away over the Welsh mountain country into England. It is like being on the roof of the world to get up them. Then sometimes the clouds come sweeping over the valley and then you are in a great white mist through which all the rocks look three times their real size. Then perhaps the mist clears a little and you suddenly see dark green valley slopes far below you and a lake shining white in the sun. It is a good place to be in."

The best way to get to know the valley is to walk along the ridges of the mountains that surround it. This walk, keeping at a height of between 2-3,000 feet, enables the walker not only to look down into Nant Ffrancon but also to see the neighbouring valleys and mountain ranges.

The walk starts by climbing Carnedd y Filiast above the Penrhyn Quarry. From above the shining slabs, with their ripple marks, near the summit one can look down into the bottom of Nant Ffrancon with Dolawen's peaceful meadow and scattered oak trees threaded by the Ogwen River sliding swiftly over a series of rapids. From here it is possible to see how the quarry slate tips have overwhelmed the lower part of the valley. The beauty one sees is what is left from a scene over which the 18th century traveller enthused. Mynydd Perfedd, the flat mountain the walker next traverses is remarkable for having a cwm on either side. To the west is Marchlyn — now a storage reservoir for Dinorwic Power Station — and beyond it Elidir — a beautiful regular pyramid of a mountain in the deeper recesses of which are the power station turbines in caverns excavated behind the disused slate quarry above Llyn Peris. On the other side is Cwm Perfedd, the hanging valley above Maes Caradoc, with its voty, its huge boulders that seem perched ready to roll down into the valley, and its peaceful pastures. Then down to Bwlch y Brecan, the quick way from one valley to another with the long grassy Cwm Dudodyn leading west to Nant Peris. Up sharply to Foel Goch, only 2,600 feet high, but with a splendid precipice broken only by grassy ledges making its summit like that of some major alp. Its peak provides a marvellous view point to look up Nant Ffrancon to the Glyders and Tryfan, and across to the Carneddau. The views, too, to the south-west across Nant Peris to Snowdon and Crib Goch start becoming impressive at this point and become even more so as the walker continues along the ridge to the next peak - Y Garn. Here the grass covered slopes down to the right to Nant Peris are not very exciting, but the whole marvellous shape of the Snowdon horseshoe across the

Tryfan from Bwlch y Brecan above Maes Caradoc.
Foel Goch is on the right. *(Photo by Steve Ashton)*

valley opens up as the walker goes south. On the left there is an excellent bird's-eye view of the succession of cwms running down to the flat valley floor of Nant Ffrancon, along with the Ogwen River meanders after its turbulent dash down the falls, Llyn Ogwen itself, running eastward between Pen yr Oleu Wen and Tryfan, comes into view — grey or blue, calm or flecked with white horses according to the wind or weather.

From the top of Y Garn more lakes can be seen. Llyn Idwal at its feet and Llyn Bochlwyd in Cwm Bochlwyd backed by Tryfan and the Glyderau. Right under the east face of Y Garn itself is a charming small lake — Llyn Clyd. To look across the valley to Tryfan from Llyn Clyd, from where a ridge cuts off sight of the valley floor, gives an extraordinary sensation of being in the high mountains.

From Y Garn to the Glyderau, the walker must go down to a broad stony saddle, varied by Llyn y Cwn and the precipitous view down the Devil's Kitchen to Llyn Idwal. From Llyn y Cŵn it is a long pull up the stony flanks of Glyder Fawr, but from there it is virtually level walking to the summit plateau of Glyder Fach strewn with fantastic boulders. Probably the best view of the Snowdon horseshoe, Nant Gwynant and all the mountains to Cnicht and the Moelwyns in the south west, is from a grassy ledge just below the Castle of the Winds between Glyder Fach and Glyder Fawr — an ideal place to camp.

From the Glyderau there are two good ways down to Ogwen Cottage. The quickest is by the Gribin — the rocky ridge separating Cwm Idwal from Cwm Bochlwyd. Coming down the Gribin one is looking straight down Nant Ffrancon with plunging views on either side into the two Cwms. Or there is a more adventurous route down Bristly Ridge which is a good scramble down rocks leading directly to Tryfan. The gullies which cut into the ridge provide short stretches of sheer rock, easily surmountable but giving the sensation of real mountain climbing. The same sensation persists after the descent to Bwlch Tryfan and the scramble up to the top of Tryfan and then again steeply down the north ridge to Llyn Ogwen.

There are two much easier ways down, either by the miners' track past Llyn Bochlwyd to Idwal or by the comparatively

Castell y Gwynt (the Castle of the Winds)
with the Snowdon massif.
(Photo by John H. Darling)

Llyn Idwal and moraines from Y Gribin.

Llyn Bochlwyd and Nant Ffrancon.

unfrequented Cwm Tryfan, with its tumbled glaciated rocks, down to the farm at Gwern-y-gof Uchaf. A more exciting route on the rim of this Cwm is to traverse the north face of Tryfan by Heather Terrace, which runs slanting across the mountain and provides the best way to the start of many of the best climbs up the Tryfan buttresses.

The round of Nant Ffrancon is completed by a steep climb from the west end of Llyn Ogwen, up Pen yr Oleu Wen, from where there is a dramatic view of Tryfan looking like a rocky fang, just across the valley, and a glimpse of two more lakes, Ffynnon Lloer and Ffynnon Llugwy, in mountain hollows. From Carnedd Dafydd the Black Ladders precipices plunge down to Cwm Llafar, the valley that runs parallel to Nant Ffrancon, and all the peaks around Nant Ffrancon stand out with a glimpse of Snowdon beyond. There is a splendid view, too, eastward towards Carnedd Llewelyn, Capel Curig and the Denbigh Moors

Aerial view of Tryfan with Idwal, Y Garn
and the sea beyond.
(Cambridge University Collection — Crown copyright reserved)

Tryfan and Llyn Ogwen from Carnedd Dafydd.

(etching by David Woodford)

Idwal and Y Garn from Tryfan
(Snowdonia National Park Authority Photo)

in the distance.

The best way down is to keep as near as possible to the skyline of Pen yr Oleu Wen so as to look down the steep precipitous stony gullies to the green floor of Nant Ffrancon. Where the rocks give way to bilberry slopes there is a sloping path above Tyn-y-maes which leads back southwards and down to the farm at Ty Gwyn, again giving one of the best views of Nant Ffrancon with Cwm Idwal in the background.

A fitting end to a long and tiring walk is to take the footpath opposite Ty Gwyn farm down to the white painted footbridge, across the Ogwen river, from which one can distinguish the small trout swimming agains the current. Just below the bridge is an eight foot deep pool, flanked by a huge outcrop of rock curved and smoothed by a glacier in the last Ice Age. A swim in this pool looking under the bridge to the line of the Glyderau in the south revives the walker wonderfully. The walk round the valley can be ended by going over a smooth rocky hump, further

View from near summit of Tryfan.
Ogwen and Nant Ffrancon.
(Snowdonia National Park Authority Photo)

evidence of the Ice Age, or direct to Maes Caradoc across the meadows, flower strewn if it is June and the sheep are up the mountain

To follow the same route round the valley in winter, when there is deep snow on the mountains and many slopes are icy, demands a high standard of mountaineering and would be difficult to complete in a day. In sunshine the mountain peaks look like the Alps against a background of deep blue sky. In stormy weather they became Artic wastes.

The ice is far more dangerous than snow and ice axes and crampons are essential. The snow cornices on the ridges of Y

Nant y Benglog from Pen Llithrig y Wrach. Gallt yr Ogof
on the left. Tryfan and the Glyderau on the right.
(Photo by Steve Ashton)

Aerial view of Llyn Ogwen and Idwal.
The main glacier came down Cwm Idwal.
(Cambridge University Collection – copyright reserved)

Garn and the Glyderau are beautiful but perilous to those who step too near the edge.

Most of the winter in the valley is less dramatic with snow on the mountains down to about 1500 or 2000 feet in cold weather, but the snow washed off by rain when milder Atlantic winds move in. Snow does not often lie for long on the valley floor, even in cold weather, but then the lakes freeze over, the ice sometimes being thick enough to walk on.

The chapters that follow are concerned with the past of these beautiful valleys comprising the Upper Ogwen, their present condition and, given modern pressures on them, their likely future over the next fifty years.

Foel Goch and Cwm Coch from Pen yr Oleu Wen.
Blaen-y-nant farm house can be seen in the valley below.
(Photo by Steve Ashton)

CHAPTER 3

From the Ice Age to the Roman Invasion

Nant Ffrancon, in its present form, is comparatively young, having been shaped by the last glacier of the Ice Age which was at its thickest about 19,000 - 13,000 BC. There was probably a winding V-shaped valley before the Ice Age started about a million years ago, with its four periods of glaciation, but it is impossible to tell how far the present valley was carved out in the three previous periods, since the last great glacier has scraped away all traces of its predecessors. The great thickness of ice in the valley, some 750-1000 feet deep, originated from the ice cap which built up a great dome over Merioneth and flowed over Snowdonia. There was a similar flow from the north west across the Irish Sea which held back the ice coming off the Snowdonia mountains, so that it piled up along the coast.

The main glacier coming over the Glyder mountains down the Devil's Kitchen, Cwm Idwal, Cwm Cneifion and Cwm Bochlwyd ground its way north down Nant Ffrancon with a branch glacier moving east past Tryfan towards Capel Curig. High up on the west side of Nant Ffrancon there were a series of tributary glaciers that dug out the cup shaped valleys which have become the cwms ranging from Marchlyn, in the north, to Cwm Clyd above Cwm Idwal. It is possible that the present mountain peaks, such as Tryfan, Glyderau and the peaks along the western side of the valley from Y Garn to Carnedd y Filiast, emerged above the ice as nunataks, that is bare rocky peaks but capable of sustaining lichen and mosses and a few alpine plants in the summer.

By about 10,000 BC the ice on the floor of Nant Ffrancon had mostly melted, but the glaciers high up in the cwms on the west and southern side of the valley were still active. Indeed, there was a renewed period of glaciation lasting about five hundred years from about 8,800 BC and it was not until about 8,000 BC, that is 10,000 years ago, that the valley and the surrounding cwms had become clear of ice. So the valley, as we see it today, is only 10,000 years old. The action of the glaciers can still be clearly seen in the crags and precipices, from which the ice plucked rocks

33

now lying in profusion in the deep cup-shaped side valleys, in the mountain lakes filling some of these hollows, and in the crescent shaped banks of moraines, particularly in Cwm Idwal, made up of small stones ground down by the ice. Sometimes the melting ice left great boulders perched precariously on steep slopes high up on the valley sides. Lower down, the great weight of ice grinding its way down has smoothed the surface of hard rocks in its way, such as the rock step below Llyn Ogwen. The rock was too hard to be worn away, but the grooves cut by sharp stones carried in the ice can be clearly seen.

The main glacier, about 1,000 feet deep, gave Nant Ffrancon its present straight U-shape, cutting away the lower part of the side valleys so that they have become hanging valleys, with streams or waterfalls running in deep ravines down the last 750 feet of steep slopes before these merge into the flat floor of the main valley. These hanging valleys or cwms all face north or north-east, since the original hollows from which they were formed allowed the snow to settle and harden into ice. This ice was not exposed to enough sunshine to prevent its building up into small glaciers, which over time plucked away rocks from the back wall of the cwms and dug out hollows, later filled by lakes. Some of these lakes are still there, though silted up; others have become bogs drained by streams which have found their way through rocky barriers at the lower end of the cwms.

Cwm Graianog below Carnedd y Filiast shows dramatically how the ice scooped out a saucer-like floor, now covered with rocks torn down from the back wall of the cwm by the retreating ice, and with a rim built up by a neat crescent shaped moraine, known as the Maiden's Arm, which looks as if it might have been a prehistoric earth work.

Cwm Idwal is an even more striking example with its precipices carved by the ice, the shattered boulders pouring down from the Devil's Kitchen, and four rows of moraines by its lake. Perhaps the traces of ice seem so fresh because they result from an active small glacier, which formed about 8,800 BC, after the previous ice had melted.

Idwal and Nant Ffrancon.
The moraines left by the glacier 10,000 years
can be clearly seen.
(Photo by Steve Ashton)

34

It was only in the middle of the last century that these evident signs of the last great Ice Age were recognised for what they were. Even Charles Darwin, recording a visit he made to Nant Ffrancon with Professor Adam Sedgwick in 1831, wrote, about 12 years later, 'We spent many hours in Cwm Idwal, examining all the rocks with extreme care, as Sedgwick was anxious to find fossils in them; but neither of us saw a trace of the wonderful glacial phenomena all around us; we did not notice the plainly scored rocks, the perched boulders, the lateral and terminal moraines. Yet these phenomena are so conspicuous that, as I declared in a paper published many years afterwards in the Philosophical Magazine, a house burnt down by fire did not tell its story more plainly than did this valley.'

There are no such cwms hollowed out in the precipices of Braich-ty-du on the south-west facing side of the valley, since it was exposed to more sunshine and there was never a chance for later, 'We spent many hours in Cwm Idwal, examining all the rocks with extreme care, as Sedgwick was anxious to find fossils in them; but neither of us saw a trace of the wonderful glacial phenomena all around us; we did not notice the plainly scored rocks, the perched boulders, the lateral and terminal moraines. Yet these phenomena are so conspicuous that as I declared in a paper published many years afterwards in the *Philosophical Magazine,* a house burnt down by fire did not tell its story more plainly than did this valley.'

There are no such cwms hollowed out in the precipices of Braich-ty-du on the south-west facing side of the valley, since it was exposed to more sunshine and there was never a chance for the snow to gather in the same way as it did the other side of the valley. There is, however, plenty of evidence of the ice of the main glacier moving down the valley scraping the steep rocky slopes high above the valley floor.

The valley floor itself would have been scraped down to the rock as the glacier ground its way down towards the north. By now the stark U-shape made by the ice as it forced its way through the rock has been softened. The rocky floor has been covered by a deep layer of stiff blue clay, left by the glacier from the stones it had ground down to dust. Later the clay was covered by a layer of lake sediment and peat built up. On the west side of the valley the steep lower slopes have been made more gentle, where they merge into the flat valley bottom, by the mantle of soil and rock washed down from the hanging valleys above. On the east side, towards the head of the valley, there are now great avalanches of boulders and scree, brought down by ice and rain from Braich-ty-du. These rock slides have gone on occurring up to the present time, when they still cut the main A5 road every few years.

As the glacier melted in Nant Ffrancon a lake was formed stretching from the Ogwen rock step as far as a smaller rock barrier at the bottom of the valley. It seems that this lake with its bed of stiff blue clay left by the main glacier only lasted as long as the rock barrier at the bottom of the valley was reinforced by the great mass of ice still pushing in from the Irish Sea, which melted later than the Snowdonia ice. So Nant Ffrancon is the only major valley in Snowdonia without a lake.

Once the Irish Sea ice melted, perhaps about 8,000 BC, the lake drained leaving the present valley bottom, much of which is still boggy in spite of the River Ogwen having been drastically dredged about fifteen years ago. The present farms in Nant Ffrancon would mostly have been below the level of the old lake. About 1947 the Electricity Generating Board put forward a hydro-electric scheme for the area which would have meant a new lake in Nant Ffrancon, flooding all the farmland in the valley bottom and at least half the farmhouses. Fortunately, it was discovered in time that the scheme would have been hopelessly uneconomic. Even with the heavy rainfall in the valley and on the surrounding mountains, there would only have been enough water to run the turbines for a few months in the year.

Once the climate had warmed up a little from about 10,000 BC onwards, tundra-type vegetation spread round the valley and up the lower slopes towards the glaciers which still kept the upper cwms frozen. According to Sir Harry Godwin plants such as tufted and meadow saxifrage grew in the valley about this time. One view is that alpine plants had survived on the mountain tops, which had been above the glaciers, and were able to take root lower down once the climate became kinder. It may be too that some of these alpines grew on rocks which were detached from the peaks by the action of ice and rolled down into the valley carrying plants with them. At the same time, alpine plants from lower altitudes followed the retreating ice up the mountain.

FROM 8,000 TO 3,000 BC

From 8,000 BC onwards the climate became warmer and drier.

By boring through the soil and analysing the pollen in the various layers of the extracted core it is possible to find out what type of tree or plant flourished on that site back to the start of vegetation after the Ice Age. Very broadly, the climate up to about 5,500 BC was dry but with a rising temperature. Then there were about 2,000 years of damp, warm weather reaching an optimum for plant growth. Thereafter, the climate became drier again but remained warmer than at present until about 1,200 BC, when it rapidly became colder and wetter than before, though, perhaps, no worse that at present.

Because the climate was benign from about 7,000 BC - 3,000 BC and, indeed, later, the floor of Nant Ffrancon was soon covered with forest made up of birch, pine and juniper which, in time, spread up the mountain slopes. By 6,000 BC there was plenty of hazel in the valley floor, pine was disappearing, being replaced by sessile oak and alder. By 4,000 BC, when the climate had become both warmer and wetter, birch had given way to oak, hazel, alder and elm. By 3,000 BC, oak, alder and willow predominated on the valley floor.

There was therefore a mixed and changing forest on the valley floor and some of the species, oak and birch in particular, and pine and juniper to some extent, grew far up the mountain slopes. Indeed, the tree line, apart from those slopes facing the sea, reached right up to 2,000 feet and, perhaps, higher. So the whole valley would have been filled with forest − the floor of the valley densely wooded and swampy − the mountain slopes covered with trees, except where there were precipices on the east and south side of the valley, and at the back of the cwms on the west side. Trees too could not have grown where the slopes were covered with rocks or scree. Thus, only the rocky slopes and the last thousand feet of grass leading up to the mountain peaks would have emerged from the forest, which in Mesolithic times − that is from about 6,000 to 3,500 BC − was frequented by animals, such as red deer, roe-deer, bear, wolf, forest horse, wild pig, elk and aurochs (the wild ox). These were the animals which had survived the Ice Age and came back into North Wales when the ice retreated from its furthest limits in southern Britain. In its forest cover Nant Ffrancon would have been like the rest of Wales and, indeed, all Britain. Unbroken forest stretched over most of the country, except where mesolithic people cleared small areas by fire and stone axes.

Up to the arrival of neolithic man, about 3,500 BC, bringing agriculture and herds of cattle, sheep and goats, Nant Ffrancon may have been visited occasionally by small hunting and gathering bands of nomadic mesolithic people. These bands have left traces in Anglesey in the form of flint tools and axes, and it is probable that they first arrived there about 6,000 BC and then spread along the present Welsh coast. Anglesey, at that time, was joined to the mainland until the rising level of the sea, resulting from the long-term effects of melting ice, finally severed the two about 3,500 BC. So people of the mesolithic era may have hunted through Nant Ffrancon or, perhaps more likely, on the edge of the forest high on the mountains where it was easier to penetrate. Their quarry were deer, bears, auroch, pig, elk and wolf. They seem to have herded the deer and auroch burning the forest in order to encourage fresh growth on which the animals could feed. While not domesticating the animals, their relationship may have been similar to that between modern Laplanders and reindeer, though nothing like so close.

There are no known traces of mesolithic people in Nant Ffrancon but it is possible that they fired some of the undergrowth, either in the valley or, more likely, high up in the mountains on the fringes of the forest.

Whether this happened in mesolithic times or not, there is evidence from pollen analysis in Nant Ffrancon near Tyn-y-maes that areas of land were cleared more than once between 2,800 and 2,300 BC because the forest had regenerated in between the clearances. It is possible that this was the work of mesolithic people who continued their way of life even after neolithic agriculture had begun to penetrate North Wales. Perhaps, and more likely, it was the work of a neolithic tribe which not only would wish to clear forest in order to make more pasture for their flocks, but to provide patches on which they could plant grain.

NEOLITHIC TIMES

Whoever first cleared land in Nant Ffrancon on the valley bottom near Tyn-y-maes, it was certainly the neolithic farmers who first made a major impact on the forest at the entrance to the valley, in particular on the high ground where, for climatic reasons, the forest was already thinning out. Indeed, it seems that the tree line had, by neolithic times, come down from its climax of about 2,200 feet to round about 1,800 feet. The neolithic invaders of Britain who reached North Wales round about 3,500 BC brought with them the agricultural and pastoral way of life which had spread across Europe from the Near East, where it had originated about 7,000 BC. Men settled in one area rather than covering great tracts of country like their mesolithic predecessors. It was these neolithic farmers who were the first to make a major impact on the forest round about Nant Ffrancon by firing certain areas and cutting others back with the help of the heavy stone axes which were, at that time, being produced at the Penmaenmawr quarry only about ten miles from the entrance to Nant Ffrancon. Once an area of forest had been cleared regeneration was slowed or stopped, either by the leaching of the soil on high exposed sites, which led to the formation of peat, or by the grazing of the cattle, sheep, goats and pigs the neolithic invaders had brought with them. So it was the neolithic farmer who first started the long process of clearing the primeval forest which was speeded up in the succeeding Bronze and Iron Ages as population grew and metal axes made tree cutting easier. But Nant Ffrancon probably did not become completely clear of trees until late medieval times. Indeed, the bog oak, the large stumps of which can still be seen in the peat in a field on the valley floor between Tyn-y-maes and Ty Gwyn, may be even more recent.

There are no traces of neolithic settlement in Nant Ffrancon, but there was a major settlement at Llandegai near the mouth of the Ogwen river five miles below the entrance to Nant Ffrancon. There are traces of neolithic rectangular houses there which can be dated to 3,300 BC. Later, it seems that two Henge-type monuments were erected about 2,650 and 1,850 BC as burial and ceremonial sites.

There is also a megalithic chambered tomb of a type common in Western Britain and Ireland, and certainly associated with neolithic man, at Fron-Deg, near Sling, on the high ground on the hills to the west of the Ogwen, not far from Penrhyn quarries.

So neolithic man certainly left traces not far from the entrance to Nant Ffrancon, and it is possible that the clearances of land that have been found near Tyn-y-maes in Nant Ffrancon dating to round about the middle of the third millennium were, in fact, the work of neolithic farmers who were clearing land for growing early strains of cereals such as hulled wheat and naked barley. There is plenty of evidence that the neolithic farmer elsewhere cleared a small area of forest and then moved on as fertility was exhaused. According to Linnard, 'The technique of shifting cultivation was that felled material would be spread and left to dry, perhaps for as long as a year. Burning would be done in one operation, probably in spring, and repeated, if necessary. Crops would commonly be sown under dead standing trees, sometimes straight into the warm ash. If tillage was necessary, a digging stick would be used.'

Clearances could also be used for providing pasture for the cattle, sheep and goats. The cattle were small animals, though apparently not as small as in the later Bronze Age. The sheep were more like the modern Soay sheep than anything else. The neolithic farmer would also have hunted, perhaps in Nant Ffrancon or on the surrounding mountains, his quarry often being the red deer or the roe-deer, which were valued not only for meat but for providing antler picks for digging ditches and other earthworks.

Whether or not the neolithic farmer used Nant Ffrancon and the surrounding mountains for his shifting agriculture and for grazing his cattle and sheep depends to a large extent on the density of population in North Wales at that time. There have been widely differing views about the size of the total population of Britain in neolithic times. But as more and more neolithic settlements have come to light in the last 25 years, sometimes because they were on the track of the new motorways, the consensus of archaeological opinion has been to push up the estimates of population in Britain as a whole.

Colin Burgess for instance takes the view in his *Age of Stonehenge* that by about 3,000 BC the total population of Britain could have amounted to several hundreds of thousands because of the favourable climate for the growth of crops and herds, even after allowing for disease and famine, which from time to time would have decimated the population. Indeed, he postulates that there was some such collapse about 3,000 BC, due, perhaps, to over-population and suggests that the clearance of forest on such sites as Nant Ffrancon round about 2,750 BC is an instance of bringing back lost land into cultivation.

If Colin Burgess is right, there could have been rather more activity in the valley than one might otherwise expect. There could also have been more people on the high ground to the north east near the entrance to the valley, since, though much of this became boggy moorland in later times, in the third millenium and, perhaps to a lesser extent in the second millenium, much of the high ground could still be cultivated. That there was plenty of land for a growing population seems to be shown by the fact that early settlements had no defensive walls.

All this is very uncertain and it would be sensible to add that even if Nant Ffrancon was visited by neolithic man at a time when the climate was considerably kinder than it is now, it is likely to have been only in the summer.

BRONZE AGE — 2,000 to 1,000 BC

Burgess puts the total population of Britain at 500,000 by 2,000 BC. It is obviously very risky to build much on these calculations, but they add support to the view that the Bronze Age was a period of considerable activity in North Wales. There is, of course, no way of knowing how far a population developed in one area rather than another, except from the number of settlements that are to be found. Here the evidence is, unfortunately, largely lacking. There are plenty of settlements to be found on the high ground to the east of the entrance to Nant Ffrancon and in the valley that leads out of Nant-y-Benglog towards Capel Curig but they have not been dated. There is firm evidence of Bronze Age activity in the shape of cairns and cists in which Bronze Age grave goods have been found. There are also many traces of hut circles and fields but these have not been excavated and may date from a much later period, for instance, Romano-British times. On the other hand it is possible that if Bronze Age people buried their dead high up on these sites, they also grew their crops there and herded their flocks, given that the climate was still favourable and a good deal of the land had been cleared of forest. We know that Bronze Age people in the second millenium pursued, though more efficiently, neolithic methods of cultivation and stock raising. With bronze axes more of the upland oak forests were felled and towards the end of the period, as the climate deteriorated, more of the forest at a lower level as well. It is therefore possible to speculate that Bronze Age farmers cultivated land up to a level of 1,500 feet, high above Bethesda on Moel Faban, in Cwm Caseg and Cwm Llafar (a parallel valley to

Nant Ffrancon) as well as on Mynydd Du, which is just on the edge of the high ground above the Nant Ffrancon. These sites have certain similarities to those 1,500 feet up on Dartmoor which have been excavated and can be dated from pottery found in them to about 1,400 BC.

It is possible too, to argue from evidence elsewhere in the country that the cairns in which Bronze Age burial urns have been found and which seem to have been linked with hut circles and field systems still visible, have been built over the field walls and thus are later than or, at least, contemporaneous with these fields. But that, for the moment, must be pure speculation. Perhaps, it would be more sensible to postulate that if, indeed, these hut circles are of Bronze Age date, the remains which can now be traced were the stone bases on which wooden posts and conical roofs were erected by shepherds who moved up to the high hills in the summer only. Such a move to the hills in the summer is, after all, the pattern of Welsh pastoral agriculture that survived until two hundred years ago. On the other hand, it is possible to take the view that the Bronze Age was a time of highly developed nomadic pastoralism, since the climate was becoming increasingly dry, which must have limited the expansion of arable farming on thin upland soils. The traces of habitation on the hills to the north east of Nant Ffrancon may have been literally camps, only visited periodically and the cairns, other than those used for burial, as indeed some certainly were, may have simply been markers indicating the grazing areas of different tribes. On this view the major advance between Bronze Age and Iron Age agriculture was the change from nomadic pastoralism to settled mixed farming.

The dating of these settlements is further complicated by the fact that some of them were almost certainly inhabited in the summer in medieval and even later times. Many, too, have been used to build sheep pens in the last two hundred years. The dating of these sites can only be settled by extensive excavation.

Given the favourable climate and population growth, some families may have made use of the lower end of Nant Ffrancon proper. The hut circles at 1,250 feet above Tyn-y-maes and at 780 feet above Pengarreg have not been excavated, but it is possible again that they were Bronze Age summer dwellings although they could have been occupied in the Iron Age. Another hut circle can be seen at Idwal, but given the inhospitable site above the Ogwen rock step where there is some of the heaviest rainfall in North Wales, it may be of a much later date and could even have been a medieval summer dwelling.

Other interesting evidence of Bronze Age activity in Nant Ffrancon and in its continuation running east towards Capel Curig has recently come to light. A Bronze Age flint barbed and tanged arrowhead was found recently near the path leading up from Llyn Bochlwyd to the pass between Tryfan and the Glyderau. At Tal-y-braich, where it has been known for sometime that there were Bronze Age burial sites, recent work has shown that there was an even more extensive activity, probably in the form of a stone circle which may have pointed to a ceremonial meeting place at the time of the Bronze Age. There are some settlements near, but here again there is no firm evidence that the settlements themselves date back to the Bronze Age. However, if there was a ceremonial meeting place at Tal-y-braich there would have been groups of people passing through Nant Ffrancon on their way from the Bronze Age settlements below the valley.

At that time there was still much wild life in the forest, such as bears, wolves and wild boar. So the Bronze Age farmers in and around Nant Ffrancon would have had to protect their cattle, sheep and goats. The cattle are likely to have been short-horned beasts, smaller than their long-horned neolithic predecessors. The sheep and goats were, no doubt, still the scrawny small Soay type which were used for milking as well as providing wool. It was in the Bronze Age that felt and, later wool textiles, began to be used for clothing, though Romans very much later found some British still clothed in skins. Horses were still hunted in the Bronze Age for food and it was not until towards the end of that time that in North Wales there is evidence of horses being used for riding in the form of bronze bits and harness. So it is possible to envisage that perhaps round about 1,000 BC, or perhaps rather later, the first riders may have made their way through Nant Ffrancon.

THE LATE BRONZE AGE AND THE IRON AGE — 1,200 BC TO THE ROMAN INVASION

Many archaeologists believe that there was a major climatic upheaval affecting most of the Old World about 1,200 BC, when a marked deterioration in the climate took place. The weather became colder and wetter, reaching its wettest period about 700

BC, and probably did not improve until the period 400 BC to 400 AD, which covers the later Iron Age and the Roman occupation of Britain. In any case, it seems that the upland fields above Bethesda may have been abandoned about 1,000 BC as the climate deteriorated further and a blanket of peat spread down the mountain slopes. If, indeed, wheat and barley were grown in Bronze Age fields rather than their being used just for cattle and sheep, it is quite possible that the land had become overcropped. As the farmers moved down and adopted a more settled life, so the forest was cleared lower in the valley.

The population was growing, in spite of the deteriorating climate, particularly by the time of the adoption of iron rather than bronze, which became general in the sixth century BC. There also seems to have been some movement of people into Wales even though the traditional view of waves of Celt invaders reaching the British Isles from Central Europe and penetrating into Wales by, say, 600 or 500 BC, bringing Iron Age culture with them, has been questioned. An alternative view is that there was no large scale invasion, although there was plenty of traffic across the English Channel in both directions. The new skills were spread from tribal territory to tribal territory into which the country was divided through what the archaeologists now call 'constant culture contact'. People thus became aware of new skills as the ideas trickled through from one territory to another. Rather than a major invasion of Celts, apparently we should think in terms of a constant dribble of refugees, traders and adventurers crossing the Channel, so that by the end of the second millenium people in Britain may already have been speaking some version of the Celtic language.

However the people round about Nant Ffrancon came to adopt the Celtic way of life, there seems good reason to believe that the population was growing and that as upland sites became unusable a land shortage developed. This would explain why some farmers moved down below 800 feet from open, unprotected hill settlements to enclosed farms with thick walls, and to hill forts, both large and small, at the mouth of Nant Ffrancon such as Pen Dinas by the Ogwen and Pen-y-Gaer below Moel Faban. Life had become colder and more dangerous. But while there was a general move to settled, mixed farming in the Iron Age, cattle and sheep round Nant Ffrancon were much more important than crops.

Recent research has shown that Iron Age hill forts were often inhabited permanently and not just in time of war. Until the hill forts near the entrance to Nant Ffrancon are excavated it is not possible to discover whether they also were always inhabited, as well as the cattle being kraaled there in troubled times.

In normal times, however, the herds and flocks would be moved out to neighbouring fields and uplands, including Nant Ffrancon in the summer, even though the valley must have become less hospitable in the colder wetter weather, which led to peat accumulating. Some of the hill forts in the neighbourhood, such as Dinas Dinorwig became quite elaborate with double walls and ditches. Both this fort and the one at Pen Dinas, which has a commanding position over the Ogwen, may have been slighted by the Romans. Pen Dinas appears to have been burnt and as a result of the great heat a part of its walls can still be seen in a vitrified form.

With widespread use of iron axes in the later Iron Age, more of the forest in and around Nant Ffrancon will have been cleared. But there was still plenty of forest left in the area when the Romans came in 59 AD, since, as is shown by their general practice in Wales, to prevent ambushes they cleared the forest on either side of the roads they built.

Apart from some forest clearance, little changed in Nant Ffrancon throughout the Iron Age and the subsequent Roman Occupation up to 400 AD. But the Iron Age settlements below the valley became the precursors of medieval homesteads and thus set a pattern of habitation that remained until the end of the eighteenth century.

CHAPTER 4

The Romans to the Tudors

The Romans, whose occupation of Caernarfonshire lasted for more than three centuries after the conquest of North Wales in AD78, left no traces in Nant Ffrancon. To the Romans North Wales was a military zone and Roman civilisation never took root in North Wales as it did in southern Britain. Nant Ffrancon would have been of little interest to the Romans, except as a way through the mountains and a source of copper.

In fact, the Romans built their main road to Caernarfon (Segontium) over the Carneddau mountains from their camp at Caerhun on the River Conwy and down to the sea at Aber. This road followed the line of a Bronze Age trackway, reaching a height of about 1,400 feet before coming down to the coast. The Romans also had a camp to the south of Capel Curig at Caer Llugwy (Bryn-y-Gefeiliau) and a temporary marching camp at Pen-y-Gwryd. They may possibly have had a route using the Llanberis Pass to join their main road running across the coastal region from Aber to Segontium. However, there is no evidence of a Roman route through Nant Ffrancon which would have been difficult because of the rock step at Ogwen and because the valley would still have been fairly densely forested. The route from Caerhun over the mountains to Aber was mostly free of forest, although it meant the unfortunate troops having to climb up a good bit higher.

There is a folk memory of a battle between the Romans and the Bodesi tribe at Pont Rhyd Goch in the Nant-y-Benglog, but this seems to have been more legend than fact. The name Maes Caradoc has been said to commemorate a Caractacus who took refuge from the Romans in Nant Ffrancon. This Caractacus (who should be distinguished from the great Caractacus who was killed by the Romans at Caer Caradoc in Shropshire) was, according to Hyde Hall in his description of Caernarvonshire, 'conjectured to have been the son of Brain ap Llŷr, called Asclepiodotus by the Romans under whom he held a command. Brain ap Llyr revolted, became a British King and was slain'. Caractacus thereupon fled to Maes Caradoc.

Although the Roman troops used Caerhun only intermittently after 140 BC and abandoned Caer Llugwy a little later, and, indeed, left even Segontium for a long period from about 300 AD because the troops were needed elsewhere, the Roman occupation brought a measure of peace to North Wales. While the natives kept to their own way of life and for the most part lived in round huts, they must have been influenced by the Roman way of life and, in particular, by Roman law. After all, the Romans were in North Wales over three hundred years, which is much longer than the British were in India. With times more peaceful and the climate reasonably good, it seems that the land above Bethesda was farmed again. Roman coins have been found high up on several sites. Some farmers around Llandegai may have grown wheat for the Roman Army taking it to Segontium in wagons along the Roman road.

It was in Roman times that horses began to be used in agriculture in addition to hunting. This followed on the use of horses in pulling chariots and the horse and chariot is quite common on Celtic coins. In North Wales it was however normally the ox that pulled the plough and, indeed, tenth century Welsh law restricts ploughing to oxen. Round Nant Ffrancon it would have been Welsh mountain ponies which from time to time replaced oxen.

By far the most important contribution made by the Romans to the life of farmers in the area was the improvement of the old Soay type of sheep by crossing these sheep, which had coarse hairy coats, with sheep with white woolier fleeces, which with further crosses, may well have led to the present Welsh Mountain breed. The resulting woolier fleece opened the way to better spinning and weaving. This process of improving the Soay sheep may well have started in England before the Romans came, as the British are known to have exported cloth. Soay sheep could only be combed while the improved sheep could be shorn. Quite when the new breed appeared in North Wales is difficult to tell.

There is no evidence that the Romans ever prospected for copper or other minerals in Nant Ffrancon, but they did establish their camp at Caer Llugwy, south of Capel Curig, in order to exploit the local lead mines and they made considerable use of Parys Mountain and the copper mines on the Great Ormes Head. There is evidence of this in the two cakes of copper with Roman stamps on them which were found on the slopes of the Carneddau above Ffynnon Llugwy. They may, indeed, have been mining copper in the Carneddau themselves.

In their time therefore, the Romans did much in building roads, in opening up copper and lead mines and improving sheep breeding. In a way this was a preview of the great changes which opened up Nant Ffrancon at the end of the 18th century. In Roman times they had little effect on life in Nant Ffrancon except insofar as sheep breeds of the new type penetrated so far into the mountains. But below the valley the Romans provided a foretaste of what was to come about sixteen centuries later.

THE DARK AGES AND MEDIEVAL TIMES

After the Romans finally withdrew from Segontium about 390 AD life became much more dangerous for the people living near the entrance to Nant Ffrancon. Irish, Saxon and later Viking invaders made life especially vulnerable for those living near the mouth of the Ogwen or along the Roman road to Segontium which crossed the Ogwen valley about two or three miles further south, and which still went on being used. They sought the protection of local Welsh princes and withdrew to the hill forts at Pen Dinas and Pen-y-Gaer in times of strife.

Nant Ffrancon itself was probably deserted for several centuries, except when used for summer pasture. But the valley may have had some more permanent inhabitants later in the Dark Ages. There is a clue in the derivation of the name Nant Ffrancon itself. Although this has often been taken to mean the Valley of the Beavers, from the Welsh word afranc, or even, as George Borrow was told when walking down the valley in 1854, the Valley of the Young Dogs (Nant Yr Ieunanc Gŵn) because of the echo from the rocky sides resembled the crying of hounds, the view of leading Welsh scholars today is that Nant Ffrancon means the Valley of the Mercenary Soldiers, from the word 'ffranc'. This could point to the first inhabitants of the valley being mercenaries paid off with inferior land by the Welsh princes they served in the innumerable wars which lasted up to the Norman Conquest and well beyond. A poem has been ascribed by William Williams of Llandegai in his *Observations on Snowdonia (1802)* to Taliesin, the famous sixth century Welsh bard, in which a battle in Nant Ffrancon is described. But this poem was certainly composed

Foel Goch
Nant Ffrancon

much later. However, there is a ninth century manuscript, a Latin paraphrase of the Gospels called the Juvencus Gospels, the margins of which were used by the scribe to include poems in Welsh. In one of these poems the hero is a warrior chieftain who has lost his companions in battle. Only his ffranc of lowly estate is with him by a camp fire.

Sir Ifor Williams' translation of the poem reads:

'I shall not talk even for one hour tonight
My retinue is not very large
I and my Frank, round our cauldron

I shall not sing, I shall not laugh, I shall not jest tonight
Though we drank clear mead,
I and my Frank, round our bowl

Let no one ask me for merriment tonight
Mean is my company
Two lords can talk; one speaks.'

Welsh princes may have paid off ffrancs of this kind who then tried to make a living on the inferior land of Nant Ffrancon and the custom may have survived into the thirteenth century.

Legend about the mountains around Nant Ffrancon have, of course, been much more powerful than what may or may not have been historically true. King Arthur, in Welsh tradition, was killed on Bwlch y Saethau *(The Pass of the Arrows)* between the peak of Snowdon and Lliwedd and Tristram's grave is on a spur of Carnedd Dafydd. Idwal, the son of Owain Gwynedd, was said to have been murdered in Cwm Idwal and his body flung into Llyn Idwal by his foster father. There is another legend that a giant's grave can be discerned in one of the moraine mounds in Cwm Idwal.

There is more truth in the accounts of the use made by medieval Welsh princes of the high mountains as places of refuge in their wars against each other and the English. Llywelyn the Great, who was probably born at Dolwyddelan Castle in 1173, and who became the virtual ruler of the whole of Wales, and not just of Gwynedd, on occasions had to retreat into his mountain redoubt. This consisted of the castle at Aberffraw, giving control over Anglesey, and the high mountains west of the Conwy river. At his castle at Aber he, and later his grandson Llywelyn the Last, were safe as long as they could get grain for their followers from Anglesey. Their flocks and herds could be concealed in the valleys running into the high mountains from the west. Nant Ffrancon and Cwm Llafar could have been such valleys. Dolbadarn Castle in the Llanberis valley was a stronghold. The redoubt survivied until Edward I seized Anglesey in 1275 and Llywelyn the Last had to agree to the Treaty of Aberconwy, whereby he was confined to Gwynedd west of the Conwy, before he revolted again and was killed at Builth in 1282.

Moving away from legend and past wars, what were the main changes in the life of those who lived in and around Nant Ffrancon between 800 AD and the conquest of Gwynedd by Edward I in 1282?

A major change would have been the further thinning of the forest, both on the valley floor and on the mountains. By the end of the period most of Nant Ffrancon valley would have been cleared and the tree line may well have been down to about 1,000 feet. In the cold and wet weather that predominated up to about 1,100 AD, the peat bogs on the mountains would have spread further down the slopes and would have thickened on the valley bottom. Cattle predominated over sheep on the pastures in the valley and on the mountain. If there was any ploughing in the valley it would have been by ox pulling a wooden plough with an iron coulter. It was the better off who used horses for riding and there was probably a track through Nant Ffrancon just as at that time there was a packhorse track up the parallel Llanberis valley.

Geraldus Cambrensis in his *Itinerary through Wales* in 1189 gives a rosy picture of its fruitfulness. 'As Mona (Anglesey) could supply corn for all the inhabitants of Wales, so could the Eryri mountains (Snowdon) afford sufficient pasture for all the herds if collected together'. But life for the ordinary Welsh people must have been hard. Geraldus recorded that they 'neither inhabit towns, villages or castles but content themselves with small huts made of the boughs of trees twisted together'. Most people in and around Nant Ffrancon lived in round huts, as described by Geraldus, but long, rectangular houses in which the cattle were housed at one end, and sometimes built on a platform, became more common as time went on and, indeed, continued to be built into the eighteenth century. It is possible that from the twelfth or thirteenth century the entrance to Nant Ffrancon at Tyn Tŵr was defended by a motte (a tower built on a mound) following the Norman pattern, rather like Dolbadarn Castle at the entrance to the Llanberis valley which can be dated to the early thirteenth century.

A further important change was the spread of Christianity which first took root in Roman times but developed in its own way when the Celtic Saints later founded missionary settlements made up of a small church and a few beehive huts, known as 'llan'. Nant Ffrancon had long been divided between the parishes of Llandegai and Llanllechid, traditionally founded by the Celtic Saints, Tygai and Llechid in the sixth century. If the primitive churches were on the same site as the present parish churches, they were several miles from the entrance to Nant Ffrancon, but there may have been a small chapel at Ty Gwyn in Nant Ffrancon by the end of the fourteenth century which conceivably could have started as a hermit cell.

During these several hundred years of rule by local Welsh princes the people in and around Nant Ffrancon formed predominantly pastoral communities of both free and bond men with common rights to grazing and arable land within wide, though defined, areas. Part of each community moved with their flocks and herds into the uplands and Nant Ffrancon for the summer following the widespread practice of transhumance. The communities were based on kindred and were regulated by detailed laws on inheritance and laying down agricultural customs and methods. These laws were later written down as the laws of Hywel Dda *(Hywel the Good).* So even though the times were very uncertain with frequent conflict between different prince princes, first against the Vikings and then against the Normans, there was a quite highly developed system of law and justice.

With the conquest of Gwynedd by Edward I and the building of castles at Caernarfon, Conwy and Beaumaris at the end of the thirteenth century, the laws changed in that English law now prevailed in the King's courts, although the Welsh law of Hywel Dda was still invoked elsewhere. The castles and the walled towns attached to them were the strongholds for rule by the English, but could have been of little interest to people living round Nant Ffrancon, except as providing a market. Welsh people were excluded from living in these walled towns and continued holding their land in kindred groups in accordance with old Welsh law.

The first documentary evidence about Nant Ffrancon dates back to the mid fourteenth century, though some of it at secondhand, in the form of the Griffith family archives which remained on the Penrhyn estate after first the Williams family took over in the seventeenth century and the Pennants in the eighteenth century. The papers are now mostly in the library of the University College of North Wales in Bangor. From these papers, James Wyatt the son of Benjamin Wyatt II and, like his father, land agent for the Penrhyn estate, produced in 1825 a map of Llandegai Parish which includes all the land in Nant Ffrancon to the west of the Ogwen river and extending to Capel Curig and Dyffryn Mymbyr, showing the land held by the different family groups (Gavels) in which land was divided equally among a man's heirs. The map was intended to show the probable state of affairs in 1352 when a major survey called the Extent of Edward III was made of the details of land holdings. But as the Welsh system of land tenure had been operating for several hundred years, it may be that this map, which is, of course, no more than James Wyatt's interpretation of the fourteenth century records available to him, takes us even further back in time.

The map is interesting in showing that Nant Ffrancon belonged to the 'Gavel Kennyn' with land stretching from Coed-y-parc just to the south of Bethesda to Llyn Ogwen. In the southern half of the holding, that is from Ceunant to Llyn Ogwen, 'Hafod Creadoc' is marked on the site of the present Maes Caradoc. A Hafod was a small building or hut in which the shepherds lived during the summer while looking after the cattle and sheep brought up for summer pasture. It appears from an unpublished thesis on the early history of the Penrhyn Estate, now in University Library at Bangor, that there was another hafod at Bryn Bryddon on the bank of Llyn Meurig, a lake at the mouth of Nant Ffrancon which later was obliterated by the Penrhyn quarry slate tips.

From the further end of Llyn Ogwen to Capel Curig there was another Gavel called Griffe with habitations of some kind (some only summer dwellings) at Gwern-y-gof Uchaf and Isaf, at Gelli, Capel Curig and Dyffryn Mymbyr. It is probable that there were permanent dwellings at Capel Curig where the church dates back to the thirteenth or fourteenth century, and at Dyffryn Mymbyr, about which there is a mortgage document of 1341 extant. Nevertheless, from Ceunant in Nant Ffrancon all the way to Capel

Curig it seems there were only five people owning land in 1352. Perhaps this is not surprising, since after two hundred years of reasonably good climate, the weather deteriorated drastically at the beginning of the fourteenth century. Indeed, there were fifteen bad harvests on end in the first half of the fourteenth century. To make matters worse, the Black Death, at its peak from 1348 to 1352, wiped out about a third of the population. With the fierce fighting of Owain Glyndŵr's rebellion of 1400 to 1410 there may well have been little further occupation of Nant Ffrancon until Henry IV imposed his peace. The powerful Griffiths family of Penrhyn were, at first, on the side of the rebel, Owain Glyndwr but submitted to Henry IV in 1407 and were rewarded with the lands of other rebels. The Rector of Llanllechid and his entire flock had already made their peace with the King in the year 1400.

Under these pressures the old system of kindred Gavel groups began to break up. Indeed, by Tudor times, one hundred and fifty years later, the Griffiths family owned all the land in Nant Ffrancon and on to Capel Curig and the whole of the Glyder range. It is possible to trace from the Griffiths family documents the replacement of the kindred system by a money economy in which the tenants paid their landlord in cash. Thus the rent of Kom Kerwyt (Cwm Cerwyd) in Nant Ffrancon was 5/- in 1413. It is difficult now to know which place was intended, but the word Kerwyt may have been wrongly transcribed for Cerwyd meaning a stag and could have referred to the Benglog area at the head of Nant Ffrancon where there are other place names referring to hunting, e.g. Llyn y Cwn — lake of the dogs. This may be an indication that the head of Nant Ffrancon was still fairly thickly wooded, since deer only disappeared about the seventeenth century when the mountain forests had been further denuded by grazing.

It was in 1413 that there is mention in the documents of a slate quarry on the west side of Nant Ffrancon and in 1415 mention of Maes Caradoc in a grant to William ap Griffith and Joan his wife, 'of all lands and tenaments including one tenament lying in Nant Ffrancon between Cwm Idwal and Hafod Creadoc . . . along with mills, wares, piscary, quarries, woods and other pertinances'. It is still possible to trace the ruins of a medieval platform house on the west bank of the Ogwen near Ceunant. It may have been the first of the Ceunant farmhouses which were on this site near the river until the late eighteenth century. Another sign of activity are the late medieval drystone walls on the summit of Carnedd Llywelyn and Carnedd Dafydd which probably marked the boundaries between grazing rights.

According to the eminent nineteenth century local historian Hugh Derfel Hughes, there was a small chapel measuring internally 16 feet by 8 feet, at Ty Gwyn, halfway down the east side of Nant Ffrancon, the last remains of which were carted away about the year 1800. There can only be circumstantial evidence for the dating of this vanished chapel, but it has been pointed out that it lies on an extension of the priest's path, the Llwybr yr Offeiriad, which runs from Nant Heilyn (near Aber) reputed to have been an early religious settlement, to Llanylchi on the north bank of the Afon Llan, said by Hughes and North to be an early church of the Celtic (as opposed to the Roman) type, and then by the Rachub side of Moel Faban, on to Ciltwllan where tradition has it there was quite a large church in the foundations of which a gold half noble of Richard II was found. The well preserved platform house nearby the site of this church is known as the priest's house. The path then goes over the shoulder of Braich Melyn, down the present sloping track to Ty Gwyn and crosses the Ogwen near Maes Caradoc before climbing up over Bwlch y Brecan to Nant Peris church, which was built in the fourteenth or early fifteenth century.

The tradition is that the priest used the path to hold services in each of these churches. The small chapel at Ty Gwyn could have been one of the places he stopped at and if, indeed, it was in existence early in the fifteenth century, as would be consistent with the age of the other churches on the priest's path, that would show there were sufficient people then living in Nant Ffrancon to warrant a service. But if there were services, it may well be that they were only held in the summer when the hafods were occupied and the weather was kinder to the priest, walking long distances over the mountains.

It seems probable that Hafod Creadoc (now Maes Caradoc) was, as its name implies, only occupied in the summer. In that event, cattle and sheep would have been driven up from a hendre, a permanent winter farmstead, lower down the Ogwen, with the cattle being more numerous than sheep. The cattle were small, active Welsh Blacks which grazed right up to the mountain tops. Sheep, also small in size, were kept primarily to produce milk for cheese to be eaten in winter. Their wool and meat were important only as by-products. The breed of sheep still had a hairy coat rather like surviving Orkney and Shetland flocks but nevertheless, they were improving in quality and had become quite distinct from the early rough type of mountain sheep, known as the Cardy. Even so, their fleece was still only half the weight of that of English breeds of the time.

One sign of more prosperous times by the middle of the fifteenth century was the building in stone of Cochwillan Hall on the right bank of the Ogwen, four miles from the sea. This splendid building, which has only recently been restored, belonged to a member of the Griffith family, which was closely linked to the Griffiths of Penrhyn.

It was only in the fifteenth and sixteenth centuries that the local landowners grew prosperous enough to build mansions in stone. Of more direct interest to Nant Ffrancon were the drovers, who had begun driving cattle out of Wales into England as early as the mid-thirteenth century onwards as and when times were peaceful enough. It is possible that the drovers began to use the rather forbidding, though direct, route through the Nant Ffrancon during the fifteenth century in spite of the disturbances of the Wars of the Roses. Insofar as the drovers did use Nant Ffrancon as a through route to England, the valley became more frequented in the summer and autumn months. By the time Henry Tudor became King of England in 1485 a more peaceful age was beginning and the valley was entering a new era.

CHAPTER 5

The Changing Valley 1500-1820

In the course of the sixteenth century the present pattern of farms in Nant Ffrancon was becoming set. Already by 1503 there is a record in the Penrhyn estate papers of ten holdings in Nant Ffrancon, for which a total rent of £12 was received. Some of the place names mentioned are now impossible to trace, but by the end of the century other records, taken together, show nearly all the present farms. One cannot tell which farms were only occupied in the summer, but it is probable that most were lived in all the year round. The population was increasing at the time quite fast and the number of single farms multiplied during the sixteenth century owing to economic inducements and the decay of the old tribal institutions. With more peaceful conditions, which came with the Tudors on the throne, farmers were moving up into the mountain valleys. Temporary summer settlements were becoming permanent hill cattle and sheep farms. The system changed over the sixteenth to eighteenth centuries from an ascending summer migration for the farmers, his family, cattle and sheep into a descending winter one for sheep alone.

There would, too, have been more traffic through the valley, along the packhorse track, following the 1536 and 1542 Acts of Union of England and Wales. The better off Welsh gentry sent their sons to be educated at Oxford or at the Inns of Court. Even the farmers of Nant Ffrancon were affected, as the number of drovers driving cattle through the valley on their way to England increased with the growing English market. Not only did the drovers provide a way of marketing cattle, for which there was not enough winter feed, but they also had to have the cattle shod in the valley before tackling the stony track over to Capel Curig. There may well have been a forge at Maes Caradoc and there was another, though probably later, by the side of the Ogwen Falls. At the other end of Llyn Ogwen the farm is called Gwern-y-gof Uchaf — meaning the smith by the alders.

Occasionally, members of parliament from the Welsh boroughs enfranchised by the 1542 Act of Union may have passed through the valley on the first stage of their journey to

Westminster, although most would have taken the coast route, in part itself only a track, by Penmaenmawr and Conwy. Although there were no great changes in agricultural methods, the appearance of the valley changed as the increased number of cattle and sheep grazed down the thinning forests, from which wolves and wild boar were exterminated by about 1600. It is probable that the valley floor was nearly clear of forest in the 16th century and first the roe deer and later the red deer, which used to graze the higher slopes, became rarer as the forest on the mountains became thinner and thinner, and eventually disappeared by about the end of the 17th century. But the open mountain above the farms remained unenclosed and, therefore, common land for another century or so. In a description written for Edward Lluyd, the naturalist, entitled *A New Account of Snowdonia* in 1693 the forests were said to harbour many pine martens, wild cats and polecats. Eagles, however, were dying out.

With no roads through the valley and, indeed, in neighbouring parts of Caernarfonshire, life remained hard for the farmer. *A New Account of Snowdonia* stated that in Llanberis parish, next to Nant Ffrancon, there was 'no cock, hen or goose, neither miller, baker or any other tradesman, but one taylor only'. It was worst of all for the labourer whose housing Thomas Pennant, writing as late as 1776, described as 'being made of clay, thatched and destitute of chimneys'. Some cottages had no door, only a hurdle and a hole in the roof served as a chimney'. The primary form of the 17th century cottage was, indeed, a single storey dwelling of two rooms, either divided by a partition or by cupboards which also served as beds. Both rooms would be open to the roof until the late 17th century when the croglofft design came in which meant there was a loft over the small room, reached by a ladder from the main living room. In Nant Ffrancon the farmhouses would have been more substantial and built of stone, of which there was plenty lying around. But the walls would have been roughly built without mortar, and it is not surprising that none of these buildings have survived the heavy rainfall and frost. The only remains of 17th or 18th century building in the valley are the foundations of a mill on an islet in the Ogwen at Ceunant, and a cottage between Braich-ty-du farm and the Ogwen Falls and the core of Blaen-y-nant farmhouse.

At least one earlier farmhouse, that at Pentre, disappeared

under a landslip. It is possible that there was more than one house here, especially as there was some mining in the area in the early 18th century. The 19th century local historian Hugh Derfel Hughes wrote that six houses were buried. The various accounts of the landslip differ as to when it happened, and it is possible there was more than one in addition to that recorded by Hugh Derfel Hughes as having taken place in 1799. According to Hyde Hall, there was a bad landslip about 1500 while local tradition dates the landslip, or, perhaps, another landslip, as about 1700.

There is also some difference of opinion amongst the experts about when sheep began to outnumber cattle in the North Welsh mountains. The accepted view until fairly recently was that cattle predominated until the 18th century. However, the *Cambridge Agrarian History of England and Wales* (1967) puts the change over earlier in the 16th or early 17th century. In Nant Ffrancon it is quite likely that sheep numbers increased faster than cattle, because the steep valley sides were more easily negotiated by sheep and goats than by even the nimble small Welsh Blacks. There would also have been the problem of feeding cattle in the winter from the comparatively meagre hay crops on the valley floor, which, though by now denuded of trees, was about two-thirds marsh. So a proportion of the cattle as well as the yearling ewes would have had to go down to lowland farms in the winter, except insofar as the cattle and some of the sheep were taken off by the drovers to meet the soaring demand from English markets.

From the 16th century onwards there was also a growing market for Welsh wool and cloth. The fact that there were two fulling mills *(pandai)* on the Ogwen river in the 16th century shows there must have been plenty of wool even then and it is quite possible that sheep and goats outnumbered cattle in Nant Ffrancon by about the middle of the 17th century. But there would have been far more cattle there at that time than are to be seen today when most farms keep no more than ten head of cattle each.

Contemporary accounts of diet in the 17th and 18th centuries make it clear that the mountain farmer hardly ever ate his own stock, whether beef or mutton. His main diet was oat porridge, sour milk, cheese and sometimes fish from the weirs at the mouth of the Ogwen river. Nevertheless, it seems to have been a healthy life for those who survived high infantile mortality, as a letter of 1690 from Meredydd Owen to Dr. Platt recounts that in "Nant Phfrancon to see men and women of seventy is no rarity; it being not unusual for such to pursue ye sheep and goats to ye steepest rocks and highest mountains". He also mentioned that Rhys ap Owen of the neighbouring valley of Llanberis was 101 and that the mussels in the Ogwen river produced pearls.

The farmer and his family would have had to be strong because, with no roads, the only vehicle available was a sledge, pulled either by men or by ponies. Edward Pugh in his *Cambria Depicta* describes how in 1804 peat was still brought down a steep mountainside on a light sledge with iron runners, pulled by a man who had to be very nimble and skilled to prevent the sledge overturning or running him down. Because of deforestation, peat was the main fuel from the 17th century onwards. Coal was far too expensive and almost impossible to transport from the port to which it had been shipped. The sloping track on the east side of the valley leading down to Ty Gwyn was used for bringing down peat and later for transporting slate. Much heavier sledges pulled by ponies were used for the sporadic quarrying of slate which took place at the entrance to the valley, to be shipped from Aber Ogwen. This must have been a most inefficient way of carting slate, since there would have been a lot of breakages. Some slate, no doubt, went on packhorses, where they perhaps had a better chance of survival. But for people in Nant Ffrancon, slate quarrying was only an occasional way of earning money and made little impact on the valley until the second half of the 18th century. Up to this time roofs were thatched rather than being slated or had a covering of sods and heather.

By the 18th century the permanent farmhouses in Nant Ffrancon mostly had their own hafods for their summer pastures high up in the cwms along the west side of the valley. Above Maes Caradoc at a height of 1600 feet in Cwm Perfedd was a hafod whose ruins still stand. It is built on a stone platform and is about 28 feet long. Life there in the 18th century must have been very similar to that described by Thomas Pennant in 1776 – "The house consists of a long, low room with a hole at one end to let smoke out from the fire which is made beneath. The furniture is very simple; stones are the substitutes of stools and the beds of hay range along the sides. They manufacture their own clothes and dye their cloths with lichen. For their own use they milk both ewes and goats and make cheese of the milk for their own consumption. The diet of these mountaineers is very plain, consisting of butter, cheese and oat bread; they drink whey, not but what they have a reserve of a few bottles of very strong beer by way of a cordial in illness. They are people of good understanding usually tall, thin and of strong constitutions from their way of life".

Of importance to the tenant farmers of Nant Ffrancon was the fact that up to about 1680 their landlords – first the Griffith family then the Williams family, including the descendants of Archbishop John Williams, were Welsh speaking, although, of course, equally fluent in English. After 1684, when the young Sir Griffith Williams died, the estate was divided between his sisters who married Englishmen, both absentee landlords. When the Pennant family acquired first half the estate through marriage in 1765 and the rest of it in 1781, the landlord lived on the estate but was no longer Welsh speaking. At that time the inhabitants of Nant Ffrancon would speak no other language than Welsh, nor had they any other opportunity to acquire English, since the nearest school which was founded at the beginning of the 18th century by Dean Jones at Llanllechid, had only ten children, and only functioned spasmodically.

RICHARD PENNANT'S GREAT CHANGES IN THE VALLEY

Life in the valley did not change to any marked extent until the second half of the 18th century. The valley could not have escaped from the great changes being brought about throughout England and Wales by the industrial revolution and improvements in agriculture, but the pace of change in the valley was greatly accelerated by Richard Pennant, the son of John Pennant, an immensely rich Liverpool merchant with several sugar plantations in Jamaica. The Penrhyn and Cochwillan estates had since 1684 been divided between the Yonge and Warburton families. John Pennant had, for a long time, been negotiating for the Yonge moiety, while Richard Pennant in 1765 made sure of the Warburton moiety by marrying Anne, General Warburton's sole heiress. Richard Pennant did not finally acquire the Yonge estates until 1785, four years after his father's death. But from 1768 the Pennant family took an active part in the management of the estates and particularly in developing quarries on either side of the entrance to Nant Ffrancon. It was Richard Pennant who brought about major changes in Nant Ffrancon by opening the present enormous Penrhyn Quarry in 1785, by exploiting other minerals in the valley such as copper, by building a road through the valley to Capel Curig in 1792 and by trying to improve the standard of farming through the conditions he attached to leases issued to tenants. Much of the credit for these developments must also go to Pennant's architect and estate agent, Benjamin Wyatt II, who actually carried them out.

In 1768, soon after the Pennants began to develop the estate, a large scale map was drawn in the Penrhyn estate office which provides a useful benchmark from which to chart the changes that came about once Richard Pennant took control. There were no roads in the valley to be shown, but nor was the course of the two tracks running up both sides of the valley marked on the map. In 1768, and, indeed, for centuries before, one of these tracks went along the route of the present "old road" past Maes Caradoc and Blaen-y-nant and round the head of the The other track ran past Tyn-y-maes and Braich-ty-du, and went up the east side of the Ogwen Falls and then along the north side of Llyn Ogwen. The usual route through Nant Ffrancon and on to Capel Curig used part of each route to avoid the stone falls from Braich-ty-du on the east side of Nant Ffrancon and the rough ground above the rock step at the head of the valley, and along the lower slopes of Tryfan on the south side of Llyn Ogwen. Edward Lluyd, the naturalist, records in 1693 "a great fall of rock from the crags overlooking Nant Phfrancon called Hysfae" (now Braich-ty-du) in 1685. A large quantity of material fell into the valley and one mass of rock "continued its passage through a small meadow and a considerable brook and lodged itself on the other side". Indeed, a large block of stone may still be seen embedded in the ground on the left bank of the Ogwen a short distance below the clapper bridge. Thus, most travellers used the track past Maes Caradoc and below Blaen-y-nant (an easier crossing than at the top of the Ogwen Falls) then crossed the clapper bridge and went up the east side of the Falls, where some of the stone steps may still be seen. Thomas Pennant called it "the most dreadful horse path in

Wales". But for centuries it took the cattle drovers and all other traffic. Just below the top was a smithy for shoeing cattle, though it is difficult to know how much it was used at this period. More likely it was used too for sharpening road making tools when first the Capel Curig Turnpike Trust road was built along the east side of the valley about 1805, and when Telford's road followed much the same course in 1818.

After skirting the north side of Llyn Ogwen, where more stone steps can still be seen, the horse track kept on the north side of the valley nearly all the way to Capel Curig.

The estate map shows all the farms now to be found in Nant Ffrancon and Nant y Benglog except for Tal-y-Llyn at the east end of Llyn Ogwen which was not built until about 1840. Some farms on the map just below Nant Ffrancon have disappeared under the outskirts of Bethesda. Tyn-y-Twr farm has gone and Penisa'r-nant which was in about 1800 to become Lady Penrhyn's dairy, was in 1768 a farm of 140 acres. Now the hill land is now mostly covered with bracken and scrub.

Ceunant (Rowland at Pen...)	a	r	p
A House yards & Caer Tŷ	2	-	4
B Bryniau	17	1	-
C Caer Bwlch gwynn	15	1	24
D Gweirglodd uchaf	5	2	18
E Cae garw	30	3	4
F Cwm y Ceunant	65	3	4
G Caer Tŷ	2	-	22
H Cae bach	1	-	16
I Gweirglodd	9	2	9
K Do	-	3	31
Total	150	2	12

Maes Caradog (Maurice & Mary Pierce)	a	r	p
A Building & Yards	-	1	27
B Gorddwn	25	-	18
C Caer Galan	15	1	8
D Gallt uchaf	103	-	-
E Cwm uchaf	150	2	-
F Ffridd Flavodly	16	3	8
G Graianog	283	-	20
H Y Gesel	24	2	-
I Cae uchaf	23	2	8
Total	642	1	9

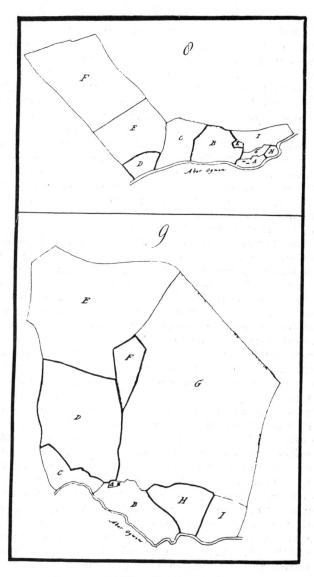

*Ceunant and Maes Caradoc Farms as on
1768 Penrhyn Estate map.*

Taking the existing farms from the north end of Nant Ffrancon, Dolawen extended right up the mountain slopes now covered by the Penrhyn quarry tips. Dolawen was remarkable in having a potato garden at a time when potatoes were comparatively rare in the North Welsh mountains, although by 1800 they had become much commoner. Then the surveyor of the neighbouring Vaynol estate advised that tenants "should not get potatoes but for the use of the family and not for sale".

Ceunant is shown as a separate farm of 150 acres with its house and yards by the banks of the Ogwen, just below Pont Ceunant, which was not built until 1846. It seems that the farmhouse was near or on the site of the medieval platform house, the foundations of which can still be seen. Ceunant was later run in with Dolawen. In 1768 it is probable that the lower end of the valley from Ceunant down to Tyn-Tŵr was denuded of trees because of the demand for charcoal and shipbuilding. The woods that now flourish along this stretch of the Ogwen were planted by the Pennants in the late 18th century.

Maes Caradoc is shown pretty much as it is now running up to the ridge formed by the summit of Mynydd Perfedd and Bwlch Brecan except that the lands added later from the enclosure of the common land running down the other side of Mynydd Perfedd to Marchlyn Mawr are excluded. The River Ogwen flowed nearer the farmhouse than at present, which would have meant the loss of a good hay meadow. The hafod in Cwm Perfedd is shown as having its own *ffridd* (enclosed field) which has long since lost its wall. Indeed, one of the most interesting points of the 1768 map is how each field of every farm is named and the stone walls shown. It is not, of course, possible to tell how far these walls were in good repair, but the line they took must have originated from the time that the farms were permanently settled. Most of the walls to be seen today were probably first built in the 18th century with some of the highest ones later during early 19th century enclosure of common land. Building these walls, particularly those going straight up steep mountain sides, demanded considerable skill, and was an investment of great importance. Although present landlords, particularly the National Trust, are encouraging the rebuilding of stone walls, over the past century more and more walls have been replaced with wire fences.

The name "Maes Cariadog" shown on the 1768 map indicates that the map drawer was no Welsh scholar. "Cariad" means love,

but there is no such form as "Cariadog", attractive though the name would be. It is, in fact, a corruption of Caradoc, as shown on the first Ordnance Survey map of 1830. But the Penrhyn estate office went on using "Cariadog" in leases and on its estate maps for a long time.

Ty Gwyn and Braich-ty-du on the east side of the valley are shown very much as they are today, with the farmhouses on the same sites. The Ogwen river between these farms and Maes Caradoc is shown as split up into several channels, which must have made for more flooding and difficult farming. Braich-ty-du, as now, had only a narrow string of fields along the Ogwen river amounting to about one-seventh of its total land. The rest is almost totally barren steep rock and scree slopes of the mountain behind. Even with the help of some mining of iron pyrites and other minerals, this must have always been a difficult farm from which to make a living.

Pentre, whose farmhouse was to be overwhelmed by a landslip 30 years later, had the whole of Cwm Idwal, while Blaen-y-nant, whose farmhouse was, as now, sited safely on a spur of rock, had all the land on both sides of the river at the head of the valley as well as the whole of Cwm Bochlwyd.

There were no buildings where Ogwen Cottage and Idwal Cottage (the youth hostel) now are, but the farms of Gwern-y-gof Uchaf and Isaf are shown on their present sites. It is possible that these farms were important in their day in that a print of 1810 shows Gwern-y-gof Uchaf having quite considerable buildings.

The first changes in the valley came even before the first road was built in 1792 as a result of exploration for copper and other minerals and through changes in the slate quarry leases, which the Pennants were prepared to grant. As early as 1760 the high price of copper, due to using the metal to protect the bottoms of warships, led to prospecting by Archdeacon Ellis of Bangor, "in the hill above the farmhouse called Ceunant and also at the riverside close to that house". There is no record that the exploration had any success, but in 1768 a lease was granted by General Warburton to some City of London merchants for "all mines, veins, grooves, ribs, beds, flatts, holes and pits of copper, lead, tin caulk and calamine, and all copper, lead and tin ore upon or under a tenement or farm called Maes Cariadog for a consideration of 5/- and one-eighth of all minerals raised from the said tenement". A similar lease was granted for Dolawen. Both leases were surrendered in 1770 because "the lessees could not see the least encouragement". In 1782 there was renewed activity at Maes Caradoc when Richard Pennant granted a 21 year lease for the same minerals. The lessees, who included the famous Thomas Williams of Llanidan, who later was accused of obtaining a monopoly of all copper supplies in England and Wales, undertook to spend £200 in the first two years searching for ores. According to William Williams of Llandegai *(Observations on the Snowdon Mountains*, published in 1802) who was agent to the Penrhyn estate, the Parys Copper Company succeeded in discovering a "flattering vein of copper-ore", probably the Gwaith mine, but it dwindled away after yielding only six tons. The same happened with other veins of copper at Maes Caradoc in Cwm Bual and above the farmhouse. The Gwaith mine was re-opened in the middle of the 19th century and for a time was successful. The ruins of the mine workings and miners' dwellings can still be seen near Tai Newyddion. William Williams mentions molybdenum being found below Blaen-y-nant and there were other workings at Pentre before the landslip overwhelmed the farmhouse.

The Penrhyn quarry slate tips have covered the copper workings at Dolawen, which became quite extensive in the mid-19th century. As for Ceunant, where arsenic ore was mined — over two separate periods — on both occasions the works had to stop because of the ill health and often early death of the workers, as well as pollution of the river. Nevertheless, the flues which radiate underground from a central furnace for producing crude arsenic from the ore can still be seen near the river at Ceunant and have proved excellent places for games of hide-and-seek. The Welsh Water Authority was until recently considering whether to build a reservoir near these workings. The presence of arsenic ore could present serious difficulties.

A more successful enterprise was the hone stone (or oil stone) quarry at Idwal just behind Idwal Cottage youth hostel. The quarry, producing hone stone for sharpening tools and even surgeon's scalpels, dates back to before Thomas Pennant's tour of 1776, when the only way of selling the product would be by loading the stones on ponies using the packhorse track. Welsh hone stones are a type of slate not quite as hard as roofing slate. There was a mill for shaping the hone stones just above the

Ogwen Falls and it is probable that the stones were in very great demand at the time of building the toll road of 1805 and Telford's road of 1818 for sharpening the roadbuilders' tools. Indeed, the forge by the Ogwen Falls, by the packhorse track, may have been used more for this purpose than for shoeing drovers' herds of cattle.

The hone stone quarry provided regular employment in the valley since it was in operation over a long period, and there were also some small slate quarries. Mining of copper and other ores seems to have been only sporadic, apart from the Gwaith and Dolawen mines in the 19th century. But cumulatively these workings must have raised the hopes, and even the standard of living, of people living in the valley. Some used the miners' track from Idwal past Llyn Bochlwyd over the eastern shoulder of Glyder Fach and down to Pen-y-Gwryd to walk early every Monday to the Cwm Dyli copper mines below Snowdon which were worked sporadically from 1800-1916. They lived in barracks there returning home the following Saturday evening. There was always a chance they would become rich by striking a good vein of ore. Moreover, they learnt how to deal with machinery and acquired other mining skills, which gave those who had to emigrate to the United States in the middle of the 19th century a better chance of earning their living.

ROADS

It was Richard Pennant's road up the west side of the valley, built about 1792, which opened up Nant Ffrancon. When continued to Capel Curig, along the south side of Llyn Ogwen and Nant-y-Benglog it provided an important link in the route which would eventually become the main road to England, instead of traffic being forced to take the difficult North Wales coast route round or over Penmaenmawr. Richard Pennant, though keen on this new route to England, was, at first, primarily interested in building a road which ran entirely within his estate to the hotel at Capel Curig he had built by Benjamin Wyatt II, a brother of the famous architects, Samuel Wyatt (who was rebuilding Penrhyn Castle) and James Wyatt, who was, in effect, the successor of Robert Adam. The hotel was built in 1798 and had ten extra rooms added a little later. It was frequented by English tourists who, prevented by the French wars from going

abroad, were flocking to North Wales and the Lake District. Books on tours of North Wales, indeed, started being published in 1770 and by the 1790s were coming out at the rate of two or three a year.

David Pennant in the 1810 edition of his father Thomas' Tours writes, "When his Lordship first came to the estate the country was scarcely passable, the roads not better than very bad horse tracks, the cottages wretched, the farmers so poor that in all the tract they could not produce more than three miserable teams. At present a noble coach road is made even beyond Nant Ffrancon and the terrors of Ben-glog (sic) quite done away with". The noble road must have been pretty rough, but Edward Pugh in a print, probably drawn about 1804 and published in his *Cambria Depicta,* shows a coach and four bowling along the road in the valley below Dolawen, then denuded of trees.

Benjamin Wyatt II was not only an architect to Richard Pennant, but also land surveyor and estate agent from 1785 to 1818. It was he who was responsible for running the estate, and for building the road to Capel Curig. He was responsible too for the new harbour at Port Penrhyn from which slate was shipped, the spendid marine baths at Penrhyn Castle, Lady Penrhyn's house at Ogwen Bank opposite the new quarries as well as the dairy at Penisa'r Nant. He also built the model village of Llandegai and forty cottages for quarrymen near the River Ogwen opposite Bethesda. He must have designed the barn at Maes Caradoc which originally had large double doors and was hence most probably a coach house. It has a simple classical facade which is not to be found in other farm buildings in Nant Ffrancon.

By 1801 Wyatt had built a horse drawn railway from the Penrhyn quarry to Port Penrhyn. According to Hyde Hall the railway not only greatly reduced breakages among the slates, but saved a great deal of manpower and horsepower – "Hitherto the slates were carried first in panniers and, subsequently, in carts which, 140 in number, took an equal number of oxen and no less than 400 horses from the pursuits of agriculture. The business is now done upon its very extended scale by 16 horses and 12 men and boys". This horse tramway was so satisfactory

Capel Curig about 1790 before Richard Pennant built his hotel and sledges were used because there were no proper roads.

that it was not replaced by steam locomotives until 1874.

Lord Penrhyn was not content with his new road through Nant Ffrancon to Capel Curig. He was also one of the prime movers of the Capel Curig Turnpike Trust, set up under an Act of 1802 to build a toll road from Llandegai up the eastern side of Nant Ffrancon to Capel Curig and on to Pentrefoelas, where it connected with the road to Shrewsbury. This road, built by 1805, came up the west bank of the Ogwen River from Llandegai before crossing by the Pont Twr (the old 17th century bridge being widened for the purpose) to join the route of the present day A5 on which the tollhouse can still be seen opposite Ogwen Bank. A new bridge, the Pont Newydd, was built over the top of the Ogwen Falls and the road, once past Tryfan, was built on a causeway to pass the farm of Gwern-y-gof Uchaf and on over the moorland to Capel Curig. This road still provides a good walking route to Capel Curig on a line between that taken later by Telford's road and Lord Penrhyn's first coach road, which has now disappeared.

By 1808 the Post Office was using this road to get the mail from Shrewsbury to Holyhead and on to Ireland. This was a considerably quicker way than the coastal route but the road had been badly built and there were complaints, particularly about Nant Ffrancon section where the gradients were steep. There were floods at Ogwen and collapses of the road down the valley, so that coaches overturned. The road was too narrow and because of poor materials and design, could not stand up to the weather. The Riding Surveyor of Mail Coaches wrote of the toll road, "It is shocking in most parts of it. Stage coaches have been frequently overturned and so have the mails. Several horses have had their legs broken – three in a week". There was apparently no proper metalled surface on the stretch between Ogwen and Capel Curig – only a right of way from which the traffic deviated. The Riding Surveyor reported in 1810 "There is no road in winter, it is over a common".

In 1810 a parliamentary committee, investigating mail routes, commissioned Telford to report what should be done about the Capel Curig and other local Turnpike Trusts, which had neither

Richard Pennant's road of 1792 at the bottom of
    Nant Ffrancon as it was about 1804.
      From E. Pugh's Cambria Depicta.

*Ogwen Bank built for Lady Penrhyn
From E. Pugh's Cambria Depicta.*

*Llyn Ogwen in 1813 — before Telford's road was built,
but no trace can be seen of the 1805 toll road.
Etching by George Wood.*

the finance nor the expertise to maintain a satisfactory road. Telford was highly critical of the narrowness and inadequate foundation of the road. He wrote, "The road from Ogwen Bank to Tyn-y-maes is narrow and very irregular with points of rock across it, on some of which I understand the mail coach has recently been overturned. From Ty Gwn to Ogwen a parapet wall of dry stones was built on the lower side, but this wall has, in a great measure, been destroyed by travellers amusing themselves throwing stones down the precipices and leaving the roads in a dangerous state". It was finally decided that a new Shrewsbury to Bangor ferry Turnpike Trust should be set up in 1818, which would be largely financed with public money. Telford was appointed as the chief engineer. His road was a great improvement on the old Turnpike road with widths between 28 stretches of 1 in 6 in Nant Ffrancon before. Road foundations were carefully built of graded stones and well designed culverts carried the numerous streams coming down the mountainside. But though Telford did his best to protect the road from rock falls, the steep slopes on the east side of Nant Ffrancon were too much for even his skills, and the A5 is still blocked by falls of rock from time to time.

The road which was open down to Bangor by 1819 was financed by tolls and a letterpost of 16d. for letters to Ireland, which remained the rate until the penny post came in in 1841. With new mail coaches which had steel springs and glazed windows, speeds of up to 18¾ miles an hour could be maintained, horses being changed every 10 to 12 miles. Tyn-y-maes had an inn at which horses were changed in Nant Ffrancon. Once the Menai Bridge had been opened in 1826, the time allowed from London to Holyhead was 32¾ hours. By 1836 it was down to 26 hours 55 minutes. The local timings were — Capel Curig 7.02 pm, Tyn-y-maes 7.46, Bangor arrive 8.20 depart 8.25, Holyhead arrive 10.55 p.m. Of course, coach traffic dwindled as railways were built, first to Liverpool by 1838, from where there was a boat to Ireland which competed with the Holyhead service, and then to Holyhead itself by 1848. But Telford's road, now the A5, came into its own again when, in the 20th century, motorcars largely took over from railways.

Pont Newydd at Ogwen carrying the 1805 toll road.
Etching by George Wood 1813

Ogwen Falls
By H. Gastineau 1830 showing Telford's bridge.

AGRICULTURAL REFORM AND THE PENRHYN QUARRY

Ever since the 15th century small farmers and farm labourers living round the entrance to Nant Ffrancon and probably in Nant Ffrancon itself, had supplemented the meagre living they could obtain from the land by working in the shallow slate quarries, which were opened up in various places. They paid normally one-eighth of the value of the slate they dug out, but often they were behind with their payments. In 1768 John Pennant tried to put arrangement on a more regular basis by issuing 21-year quarrying leases to 54 of his tenants, including some in Nant Ffrancon. These long printed leases, which the Welsh speaking tenant would have had great difficulty in understanding as there was no Welsh translation, allowed them to have the liberty of the quarry, that is to take slates for an additional payment of 20/- a year. The slate was to be quarried on the common above the present Penrhyn quarry.

When Richard Pennant took over the estate in 1781 he was convinced that this method of quarrying, using casual labour, was very inefficient and, therefore, he bought out the 54 lessees and started running a new quarry on the site of the present Penrhyn quarries employing labour direct himself. Most of this labour would have been full-time.

New agricultural leases were granted in 1790 to many of the Penrhyn estate farmers, including those in Nant Ffrancon. These were 1-year leases, to be renewed from year to year. Although formally the tenant had less security the leases were, in fact, renewed over a long period. Moreover, the tenant had the right to compensation when he finally left for any improvements he had carried out. If, as must often have been the case, the tenant had not got the money for improvements, the landlord provided it in return for adding 5% to the rent. The other clauses in the leases were a curious mixture of old feudal customs and the then up-to-date views about limeing of fields and the rotation of crops. The tenant had to provide a horse and cart for the landlord or do three days manual work, or pay 5/- for each day team work and 3/- for each day manual work. He also had to use the landlord's mills for corn and fulling of cloth, or pay a fine. He had to undertake to lime his cultivated fields and allow them to lie fallow under clover every third year. He was not allowed to keep goats unless he paid a penalty of 5/- a day, which could

Llyn Idwal
By H. Gastineau 1830

have amounted over time to a huge sum. He was only allowed to take one hay crop a year.

These were again printed leases in English, on which the tenant normally made his mark, being illiterate. How far he understood all the conditions it is difficult to know. Perhaps this did not matter in Nant Ffrancon because there was probably only a little oats grown in the valley. So rotation of crops did not apply. It would, in any case, have been impossible to take two crops of hay a year. Indeed, the harvesting of one crop was difficult enough, since so often heavy rain meant the hay could not dry. Without any roads in 1790 it would have been impossible to cart lime, and even when the road to Capel Curig was built in 1792, it only served the west side of the valley. There were only footbridges over the river. Perhaps, after the toll road was built in 1805 on the east side of the valley, some of these clauses became operative.

As for the goats, they remained in the valley and, indeed, have survived to this day. William Williams, Lord Penrhyn's agent, describes in his *Oservations on Snowdonia – 1802*, how in Cwm Bual (and the other Cwms on the west side of Nant Ffrancon) "are the summer leys for horned cattle and mountain horses, the surrounding cliffts being inhabited by sheep and goats". At that time farmers welcomed goats, not only for the milk they provided, but because they could safely eat the grass on narrow rocky ledges high up on precipices, on to which a sheep might be tempted to jump and then find itself unable to get off again.

So while Richard Pennant's model leases were unlikely to have had any effect, anyhow in the short run, on farming methods in Nant Ffrancon, his great contribution was the provision of roads and the well built stone walls which Hyde Hall mentioned as seeing in 1810. According to his account, these walls were 5 feet 9 inches high and flat stones were laid across the top of the wall to prevent sheep getting over. Another important effect of Richard Pennant's agricultural policies were the planting of 600,000 trees between 1780 and 1797. No doubt most of these trees would have been below Nant Ffrancon, but some may have been planted round the 40 whitewashed quarrymen's cottages, designed by Benjamin Wyatt, built on the west of the Ogwen River on a site to be overwhelmed by the slate waste tips by about 1845. Many more trees were planted between Ogwen Bank and Ceunant at the turn of the century to protect the house built for Lady Penrhyn and her model dairy at Penisa'r Nant.

In 1794 George Kay, working for the Board of Agriculture which was then a voluntary society with some Government subvention, remarked in his General View of Agriculture that Caernarfonshire "once encumbered with woods was now left naked and bare, except around gentlemens' seats". Kay, whose evidence is not, perhaps, very reliable, since he made only a hurried visit to the Caernarfonshire mountains, maintained it was no longer true that whole families went up to the mountains in summer to attend their flocks and make cheese. He stated that only the wether sheep went up the mountain. The ewes, he said, were kept on low ground and ewes' milk was mixed with cows milk to make cheese. Kay also maintained that the drovers were against improvements of the cattle stock because the droving trade was in a few hands only and, if the quality of cattle went up, more drovers would be attracted in and, with more competition, they would have to pay the farmers cash for their cattle rather than buy on credit.

Farm labourers, he recounts, were paid five to seven guineas a year with bed and board, and worked a 12-hour day except in winter, when they had to work whatever hours of daylight there were. Many Methodists, he wrote, asked for lower wages in return for time off to hear itinerant preachers.

However accurate George Kay was, his book if of interest as being, in effect, a modern Green Paper, printed with extra wide margins on which the reader was asked to write his comments and return the book to the Board of Agriculture as quickly as possible. In the introduction Kay wrote these "reports are printed and circulated for the purpose merely of procuring additional information, and of enabling everyone to contribute his mite to the improvement of the county".

Walter Davies' General View of Agriculture in North Wales, published in 1810, was a far solider work based on ten years' work. The Caernarfonshire Agriculture Society in which Richard Pennant played a big part, had been founded in 1807. When the demand for slates fell off in the war with France in the 1790s, Walter Davies records that quarrymen who were thus thrown out of work, were employed by Lord Penrhyn, not only to build roads, to construct the harbour at Port Penrhyn and the railway from the quarry down to the harbour, but also to enclose and improve a large tract of very poor turbary soil above the Penrhyn Quarry which was laid down to grass to feed the cottagers' cows. The possession of three acres of land and a cow was a good recipe for a contented quarryman, particularly when employment fluctuated. He wrote "These cottages and improvements have given variety and life to a most dreary and forlorn waste. The architect giving full scope to fancy has studiously varied a plan of each cottage; plantations were everywhere judiciously grouped".

Writing also in 1810, Hyde Hall describes Ogwen Bank as "A very beautiful place, for once protected, decorated and almost hidden by its recent plantations... the greenness and lively floridity of the plantations give the place the character of an emerald set in the waste". Of the plantations round Lady Penrhyn's dairy, he wrote, they "are particularly delightful and have been introduced with so much spirit that considerable spaces of naked rock have been covered with earth for their reception".

According to Walter Davies, Lord Penrhyn erected sheds on the Llanllechid hills below Nant Ffrancon to provide shelter for sheep in winter. This example was not, as far as I know, followed at the time and is still resisted by sheep farmers today. The trouble is that if sheep are brought under cover in winter, they have to be fed which means growing more hay in summer. Benjamin Wyatt, in an appendix to Walter Davies' book, advocated the growing of more winter food so that sheep could be protected and lambing made safer. He complained that "At present, if the mountain farmer summers upon his pastures as much stock as the land is capable of maintaining, he must be under the necessity of procuring a winter run for at least one-third of his stock; and even then in severe winter, many of his sheep will die and those which survive, as well as the cattle, are a stunted sort, owing to want of shelter and good food, having nothing given them save a poor insipid kind of hay".

So Richard Pennant seems to have had little effect on the conservative ways of Nant Ffrancon farmers. But he left their farms in better state than he found them, by ensuring the walls and farm gates were properly maintained, by the provision of roads, and by some improvement in farm buildings, though it is difficult to tell now precisely what was done, since most of the farmhouses were rebuilt in the middle of the 19th century.

Nant Ffrancon farmers may have been interested in the sheep shearing competition organised by the Caernarfonshire Agricultural Society, but not in ploughing matches or in the use of the new root crops. As time went on, improvements which, to some extent, were demonstrated in the standard of building, particularly of cottages, came from the additional income from quarrying and mining rather than from cattle and sheep farming, which nevertheless benefited from improved communications. The Penrhyn estate provided £25 worth of materials for the building of cottages, which the tenant himself had to erect, and to pay 10/- a year for a 30-year lease. But they were good cottages made of slate, stone and granite, and not the miserable hovels that existed before. The present cottages at Maes Caradoc may (since they are mentioned in the Penrhyn Estate lease) date from 1813 but they were probably built about 1830.

Cattle and sheep farming, nevertheless, benefited from improved communications. Cattle no longer had to be slaughtered at the end of the summer as there was a market for meat all the year round from the growing English cities, and cattle continued to be sent there on foot until the railways took over in mid-century. The cattle were also fed on improved root crops of the lowlands and there were some improvements in the quality of grass and hay grown.

CHAPTER 6

The Quarry and the Penrhyns 1781-1914

Thomas Pennant in his Tours described Nant Ffrancon in 1776 — "This bottom is surrounded with mountains of a stupendous height, mostly precipitous; the tops of many edged with pointed rocks. I have, from the depth beneath, seen the shepherds skipping from peak to peak, but the point of contact was so small, that from this distance they seemed to my uplifted eyes like beings of another order floating in the air". His son, David Pennant, editing a new edition of his father's book in 1810, refers to "Ogwen Bank, the slate quarries, well constructed railways and the great and various improvements effected by the late Lord Penrhyn in this previously desolate tract of Nant Ffrancon".

While the writers of the numerous travel books on North Wales continued to take a romantic view of Nant Ffrancon, though many stressed its "avernian gloom" and "precipices super-eminently horrible", the most obvious impact of Richard Pennant's super-abundant energy were not at all romantic. This was the complete transformation of the north end of Nant Ffrancon as the new Penrhyn Quarry above Dolawen bit deeper and deeper into the mountain and the waste tips grew in size, until eventually they came right down to the Ogwen River. Even more important for the inhabitants of Nant Ffrancon was that, as employment built up in the Penrhyn Quarry and in smaller quarries on the other side of the river, Bethesda, named after the chapel built there in 1820, grew by 1870 into a town of about 6,000 inhabitants. Although Telford had built his road on the right bank of the Ogwen through the fields and wasteland, which later became Bethesda, without the quarries there would never have been more than a small village on that site. The Penrhyn Quarry also, by providing stable employment in most years, offered to the farm labourers of the valley at least the opportunity of supplementing their income from sheep farming.

Nant Ffrancon from Coetmor in 1813
before Bethesda was built.
Etching by George Wood.

A man could both work in the quarries and run sheep on the mountain. He could be both a quarryman and a shepherd. As a result, a number of cottages were built, particularly in the northern end of Nant Ffrancon at Maes Caradoc, Tai Newyddion, Tyn-y-maes and Ceunant, the inhabitants of which were shown in the census returns as quarrymen. These men did not have small holdings like a number of quarrymen below the quarries, but they would almost certainly have earned extra money by helping the sheep farmers of the valley at times of peak activity, such as shearing and gathering. Although the quarrymen tended to form their own close community separate in outlook from most of the farmers, the families in these cottages in Nant Ffrancon formed an important link between the two communities. Moreover, the farmers went to the chapels which sprang up in Bethesda until the first chapel, Bethel, was built at Tyn-y-maes in 1843 and the second there, Capel Saron in 1860 – with a third at Pont Rhyd Goch in 1853. Bethesda, too, provided the only school in the neighbourhood and was a convenient market for the farmers' produce.

Employment at the Penrhyn Quarry built up quickly soon after Richard Pennant took over command in 1781. By 1790, when he was created Lord Penrhyn, about five hundred men were working there. Although there was a check during the Napoleonic Wars because building throughout the country slackened and a 20% tax was imposed on coastwide shipping of slates and coal, there was a good recovery after the peace of Amiens in 1801, and by Lord Penrhyn's death in 1808 the quarry was bringing in £7,000 a year.

The quarrymen were paid more than agricultural labourers and, according to Hyde Hall writing in 1810, achieved a much higher standard of living. "Their houses are well furnished, and a clock, a chest of drawers, presses for clothes, crockeryware and pewter, all shine in their respective places; and their beds are rendered weatherproof in this boisterous region being boarded above and on three sides so that it resembles a sort of trunk". Their clothing, both for common occasions and for Sundays and festivals, are clean, whole and abundant; and with food they're equally well supplied". Hyde Hall, because of his friendship with the Pennant family, probably saw the quarrymen's life through rose coloured spectacles, or at least through those of a teetotaller, since he wrote, "but if these people eat so well, they drink still better, for they drink almost exclusively water". He admits, too, that they do not seem to drink enough milk even though it was a favourite form of food.

By 1820 employment at the Penrhyn Quarry had increased to 900 and it is at this time that the quarrymen started building their cottages on the site of what was to become Bethesda, and which at that time boasted no more than an alehouse. The land on which they built their cottages was owned by two substantial yeoman farmers, who, unlike Lord Penrhyn, were ready to sell or lease building sites without acting as benevolent despots and without any prejudice against the building of chapels or, indeed, of more alehouses.

By 1827 Lord Penrhyn's successor, George Hay Dawkins Pennant, had grown so rich from the quarry and his extensive trade in slates that he was able to commission Thomas Hopper to build the huge neo-Norman Penrhyn Castle that now belongs to the National Trust. The vastness of the building and heaviness of the elaborate oak doors and woodwork pointed to the gap in wealth between employer and employed becoming wider yet.

Mr. J. Roose Williams has pointed out in his excellent book on William Parry, the quarrymen's leader in the second half of the 19th century, that "The quarry workers formed a distinct community, almost wholly Welsh in nationality and language and non-conformist in religion". The quarrymen were separated from their landlords, the Pennant family by "triple barriers of nationality, language and religion". The same barriers existed between the farmers of Nant Ffrancon and their landlord, but the quarrymen, particularly those without any attachment to the land, formed "a new industrial class which, as yet, was neither proletariat nor wholly peasant, which lived its own separate life centred round its chapels and with its own distinctive cultural and religious interests". This culture based on a keen interest in the Welsh language, in singing, in poetry, in religion and preachers and literary criticism, was in some ways narrow but had real vision. The quarry as well as the town of Bethesda held its own Eisteddfodau at regular intervals, so that the quarry was in itself quite an important cultural centre. If the standard of poetry, singing and discussion was not always very high "it is true that the quarrymen generally had an obsession which involved discussions, a talent for dry anecdotal humour as well as for buffoonery and practical jokes, and a huge appetite for a diet of alliteration and rhymes".

This astonishing amount of activity was in the quarry organised through the *cabans,* – stone huts on the ridges between the quarry working faces which served as the quarrymen's canteens. Here, while eating and resting in the middle of the day, formal meetings were held with a chairman and secretary, so that the *caban* was, in effect, a debating chamber, a test of literary skill, and later a trade union office. The meetings were by no means always serious. They were an opportunity for humerous verse and for a great variety of different word games. But they were also the place for airing grievances, for organising money-raising concerts to help colleagues, who were ill or hurt in accidents, and to look after their families.

Apart from the documentary evidence about the specifically Welsh culture of the quarrymen contained in memoirs and in the minute books kept by some cabans, visual evidence has recently been brought to light by the Llandegai and Llanllechid Archaeological Society, which has collected a lot of the large carved slabs of slate which surrounded the fireplaces in the new stone built cottages, particularly those built in the prosperous times between 1823 and 1843, a period which coincides with the trebling of the workforce at Penrhyn quarry. New houses were built, and others refurbished, with carved slate slabs measuring 7½ feet long for the horizontals and flanked by two slightly smaller uprights round the kitchen grate. The most frequent pattern for the carvings was made up of concentric circles, but there were many carvings which were far more elaborate, showing daisies and other plants, fish, birds, different types of buildings and cottages, churches and castles, furniture, clocks, hearts, ships, bridges and musical notation. These designs were carved free hand and have a freshness and sometimes a naivety which is most attractive. Some of the carvings by quarrymen who normally worked a 12-hour day, showed not only great pride in their cottages and growing prosperity, but a great desire to learn. At a time when education was hard to come by, groups of quarrymen set up their own schools to learn musical notation. Some of their slates show their mastery of the subject. Other carvings are intricate and show a great ability to understand astronomy and mathematics. One quarryman, John Williams Thomas, who went on later to work at the Greenwich Observatory, made the drawings for an elaborate slate carving

Carved slate fireplace in Gerlan, Bethesda about 1830
Photograph by Martin W. Roberts.

Telford's Menai Bridge and the steamer Prince Llewelyn

Further detail

explaining the eclipse of 1836 and the movements of Halley's Comet as well as the relative size of the planets. Thomas was an exceptional man who, after three years of schooling and seven working in the quarry, had educated himself enough to become a teacher and write a number of books, one on the elements of mathematics and another on grammar entitled *An Infallible Way For A Monoglot Welshman To Read English Correctly*, which involved the use of phonetics. But the two other quarrymen who actually carved the slate with this astronomical detail showed an extraordinary high degree of skill and sense of design. Similar carved slates have been found in other North Welsh slate quarrying districts, but on the available evidence, the art reached its zenith in the Ogwen Valley. Many of the carved slates show a date but none are dated later than 1843. This was because tastes changed as the quarry mills began to make slate fireplaces of a very different kind, deeply carved with rosettes and columns, by skilled men employed specially for the work rather than by individual house proud cottage holders. Moreover, the Victorian fashion of attaching bobbles and fringes, and hanging plates under the mantlepiece, would have covered up the carvings on the horizontal slate slab over the fireplace.

Four hundred examples of carved slates have been found in the Ogwen Valley and there must have been a great many more, allowing for the subsequent demolitions or, at least, radical changes in modernizing cottages over the last 140 years since the carved slates went out of fashion. The carved slates were mostly to be found in Bethesda and neighbouring villages down the Ogwen Valley, but a few have been found in Nant Ffrancon at Tyn-y-maes and Maes Caradoc. An ostler at Tyn-y-maes called William Roberts, after attending Robert Williams' school of music, mainly for quarrymen, at Carneddi, became the best musician in the valley. He composed the well known hymn tune *Andalucia* in 1830, called after a favourite coach horse he groomed. Thanks perhaps to William Roberts carved slates found in Nant Ffrancon display simple tunes.

These slates provide therefore some good evidence that for the house proud quarrymen, at any rate, the standard of living was higher than many of the contemporary written accounts of working class life would lead one to suppose. They showed good furniture, grandfather clocks and corner cupboards. There are slate plinths to lift the best furniture off the earthern floor and these plinths are carved as well as the pieces of slate which stand between the feet of the dressers or clocks to prevent dust accumulating underneath. These particular cottages were certainly not dirty hovels. As long as they were in employment these quarrymen most probably had good fires of wood, peat and coal on which to cook, though kitchen ranges came in later.

THE PENRHYN QUARRY AND NANT FFRANCON

The population grew fast in and around Bethesda in the first seventy years of the 19th century, from about 2,600 in the 1801 census to 11,800 in the 1881. This was largely due to employment at the Penrhyn Quarry reaching 1600 by 1835 and 3000 by 1863. Most of the quarrymen lived in Bethesda itself, which reached a peak of 7,700 people in 1871. But many more people were living at the north end of Nant Ffrancon than before or since, thanks to employment available at the quarry. So the influx was almost entirely due to quarrymen and their families living in newly built cottages at Ceunant, Maes Caradoc, Tai Newyddion and particularly Tyn-y-maes, where the total population had reached 100 by 1841, of which 28 were quarrymen and only eight agricultural labourers. The total number of quarrymen there grew to 37 by 1861. At Maes Caradoc, of which Tai Newyddion was then part, were housed five families of quarrymen and one agricultural labourer in 1841 in addition to seven people living in the farmhouse. By 1881 there were seven households there totalling 39 people, of which nine were quarrymen. Even Braich-ty-du housed four quarrymen out of a total of 14 people as early as 1841. In all there must have been about 250 men, women and children living in the northern end of Nant Ffrancon as against less than 25 now. There were more people, too, in the eastern end of Nant y Benglog as there were agricultural labourers living on nearly all the farms. Owing to fluctuations in employment at the Penrhyn Quarries, numbers in the valley began to fall by the 1881 census, but the two cottages next to Maes Caradoc farmhouse housed between them eleven men, women and children. Only after the disastrous Penrhyn Quarry Lock-out of 1900–1903 were more and more of the quarrymen's cottages deserted.

In the 19th century, with so many more people living

permanently in the valley, the whole atmosphere must have been quite different, especially in the winter, even though in that wide landscape people are always dwarfed by the steep mountainsides and the great open spaces of the flat marshy valley bottom. Now it is only in the spring and summer months that the loneliness of the valley gives way to holiday-makers. But, of course, there is always a stream of traffic down the A5 now, while in the 19th century there would have only been occasional coaches and carts, as well as quarrymen walking to work.

It was these quarrymen who kept everyone living in Nant Ffrancon deeply concerned about the conflicts which arose at the Penrhyn Quarries between the quarrymen, many of whom joined the North Wales Quarrymen's Union after it had been formed in 1874, and the aristocratic English Penrhyn family whose handling of a difficult situation ranged from benevolent, though despotic, understanding, to total failure to even try moving with the times. The quarrymen's employer and the farmers' landlord was the same man, Lord Penrhyn, who was immensely rich and politically powerful, both in local and national politics. Some farmers were, moreover, dependent on the quarry to be able to keep their farms solvent. Although the detailed evidence to the Royal Commission on Land in Wales and Monmouthshire in 1894 was about neighbouring valleys, they are highly relevant to life in Nant Ffrancon. One farmer's son said, "In my father's time I worked at the quarries, and used to hand over the whole of my wages to my father to assist him to live and to pay the rent and rates... In the summer months I used to work upon the farm after returning from the quarry until it was too dark to work". Another witness told the Commission that the farmers "get assistance in certain parts of the year in the quarries to pay their way, and amongst many of the small farmers I think they work in the quarries to be able to pay rent for these farms. If it had not been for the quarries they could not live on the farm".

While farmers and quarrymen often had similar economic interests and both came from the same Welsh speaking, chapel-going community, there were differences in outlook between them. These developed as the quarrymen's community, especially in Bethesda, became more closely knit, and, under the pressure of strikes and lock-outs, more radical, while the farmers tended to be more conservative and ready to criticise the

Bethesda quarrymen's way to life. To some extent this was the difference between the countrymen and the town dwellers' outlook.

Throughout the 19th century the quarrymen developed their own special way of life, which as time went on differed more and more from that of the farmers living in Nant Ffrancon or in other neighbouring valleys. The quarrymen outnumbered many times the farming community, there at one time being 3,000 employed at the Penrhyn Quarry at the bottom of Nant Ffrancon and an equal number at the Dinorwig Quarry at the bottom of the Llanberis Valley. The main distinctions, apart from the intensive cultural life of some quarrymen that has already been described, was in dress, diet and health.

While, in the 20th century the quarrymen wore the usual corduroy trousers, hobnails boots and flat cap of many labourers, in the 19th century the quarrymen's normal dress was of white fustian with "a thick flannel vest, a flannel shirt, generally lined, flannel drawers, usually double thickness round the waist, and in addition he generally also wears round the waist a flannel belt or bandage". (Report of the Quarry Committee of Enquiry 1893). In addition, the 19th century quarrymen on his way to work invariably wore a bowler hat and carried an umbrella.

The quarrymen's diet and state of health attracted much adverse comment from the numerous enquirers of the Victorian age looking into social conditions. They were said to be the worse fed men of any class in the kingdom, though their wages were above that of agricultural labourers and many other people working in the country. The general medical verdict was that the quarrymen drank too much tea and ate very poor food. Heavy tea drinking appears to have been a particular characteristic of the quarrymen — "tea for breakfast, tea for lunch, tea for tea and tea for supper" complained Dr. Jones of Penygroes. The tea they drank was, moreover, brewed in a particular, and in doctors' eyes, harmful way for it was a normal habit "of the quarrymen to send a boy about half an hour before the mealtime to an eating house, prepared by the owner for their comfort, with tea and sugar and water in the same kettle, which is put on the fire and boiled, then stewed there for half an hour or more before the men come to drink it".

The constant drinking of tea apparently made up for the scarcity of nourishing food in the quarrymen's poor diet, which typically consisted for the majority, (that is for the quarrymen who did not look after themselves) of tea and bread and butter for breakfast, and same for dinner, tea and supper, though sometimes "he may have in addition a little cheese, potato or bacon.... this is the exception".

An English cooking instructress in Blaenau Ffestiniog reported that "they only seem to get meat once a week and that on Sunday". They seemed to eat no vegetables or anyhow not enough, and consumed little dairy produce such as milk. In terms reminiscent of modern medical advice, Dr. Roberts compared the quarrymen's diet unfavourably with that of agricultural workers who eat "good, coarse flour which is much more wholesome. The quarryman, on the other hand, eats too fine a flour". This seemed to show that the quarrymen's diet was a matter of preference, since they could have got more wholesome food which would have been cheaper. That some quarrymen's families did have a good healthy diet is shown by letters written by Hugh Derfel Hughes. But of the majority, as Dr. Roberts pointed out, although "they could get plenty of sweet milk or buttermilk to drink, they have got into the habit of drinking tea at every meal. They have no relish for any liquid except tea, it is tea all day long". Indeed, there was a special tea packaged locally and marketed under the label The Quarrymen's Tea.

Giving the long hours of work at the Penrhyn Quarry, 6.30 am to 5.30 pm on weekdays and 6.30 am to 11.30 am on Saturdays, most of it carried out either out of doors in the damp, and often in heavy rain, or indoors in the slate splitting shed, full of dust, it is not surprising that the quarrymen's health was poor. The most serious complaint was respiratory disease − silicosis − mainly due to slate dust, though the weight of medical opinion at the time suggested that poor living conditions rather than occupational hazards was the main cause of poor health. The death rate statistics for quarrymen of different skills pointed to the danger of slate dust. Those employed in the splitting sheds where the slate dust was most heavy had an average age at death of 48 years. The average age of death for engine drivers and plate-layers in the quarries − those least exposed to slate dust − was 60 years. Those who hewed the rock from the quarry walls and hence were again subjected to slate dust − that is the rock men and miners − did not live, on average, much beyond 48 years.

The quarrymen themselves were good at organising sick clubs and Lord Penrhyn provided a hospital at Bethesda in the 1860s. But this was not enough to offset the poor working conditions and occasionally inadequate care which some quarrymen were said to have received from their wives.

Quarrying is, of course, a totally male industry and in Bethesda, where it was by far the chief source of employment, there was very little work for women. Indeed, in Bethesda of 2,289 women over 10 years of age in 1901 83% were not in employment. Of the rest who were, there were 141 domestic servants and 117 tailoresses. The alternative to work was marriage and thus marriage tended to be early. It is said that some women of the quarrying villages, including Bethesda, confined as they were to the house, developed a way of life which according to the inspector of mines in 1875 cannot have made for a happy home. He wrote, "The wives lack thrift, know nothing of cooking and spend a large proportion of their husband's earnings in the purchase of gaudy finery, for which they are seldom free from debt. The men therefore fare badly ... their homes are as comfortless as slovenliness can make them". The wives were said to prefer making "pancakes swimming in butter than a proper dinner", and that they would gossip all day and then open a tin when their husbands arrived home from work rather than cook a proper meal. These criticisms can hardly be substantiated. Against them there is plenty of evidence of thrifty hardworking quarrymen's wives determined to do the best for their children. The wives, after all, must have had a hard time running their rather damp houses and cottages, not only for the husband but for numerous children. There were no labour-saving aids then. T. Rowland Hughes, in his novel *William Jones* provides in Leusa a cruel caricature of the lazy and extravagant quarryman's wife. However, Leusa is contrasted with the hard working and caring wives of most of the other quarrymen. It may be that some of the criticism came from women working on surrounding farms. On the land women played an important role in farming, while in the terraces of the slate town women's work was almost exclusively in nursing and domestic and charitable work in helping sick quarrymen's families and their widows. In such circumstances, an interest in appearances, both of themselves and their houses was to be expected. It was not, perhaps, that they were slovenly. Rather they had an obsession with cleanliness and the collection of furniture and ornaments which were constantly polished, while being kept in the front room, which was hardly ever used. According to a contemporary account, they had to have a piano and they "must get a grandfather clock as large as Goliath's coffin worth 8 guineas; an 8 guinea glass cupboard for their trinkets; 8 guinea dresser moaning under the weight of crockery, as well as of china, dogs, cats and soldiers, and in between them all there was no room for the quarrymen to turn".

This was an unfair exaggeration, but it does show that some quarrymen's families had a standard of living well above that of the small farmers in Nant Ffrancon.

There is a picture in Jean Lindsay's book, *A History of the North Wales Slate Industry,* which purports to illustrate a meeting between Lord Penrhyn and the Penrhyn Quarry Committee in 1874. Lord Penrhyn, as one would expect, is dressed in a frock-coat complete with silk stock. William Parry, the quarrymen's leader at the time, is similarly dressed and has a well polished silk top hat on his knees. The quarrymen are standing, but they are all likewise dressed in frock-coats, albeit without silk stocks. Instead they wore bow-ties. All had waistcoats and some had watch chains. Whether the picture is an accurate representation one cannot tell, but it is quite possible that the quarrymen's leaders made a point of dressing in the same way as the gentry so as to try and be on level terms. The better-off quarrymen with positions in the chapels as preachers, possessed formal dress which, indeed, contrasted very strikingly with their working clothes. Early wedding photographs demonstrate this – as does the custom of Sunday clothes being kept pressed during the week with the help of heavy slates. It must have been pretty certain that no Nant Ffrancon farmer would have had such an outfit.

Some quarrymen had enough spare cash to invest, usually in local shipping. The Bethesda Shipping Company formed in 1862 had 249 shareholders. Many quarrymen were concerned about education and contributed a penny a week out of their wages in 1884 towards the founding of the University College at Bangor. The total subscription amounted to £1407, and even today, we are often reminded that the university was built with the "quarrymen's pennies".

TROUBLE AT PENRHYN QUARRY
– THE STRIKES AND LOCKOUTS OF 1865–1903

By and large relations between the quarrymen and the successive Lords Penrhyn up to 1885 were reasonably amicable in spite of conflicts about the level of wages and the right of the men to elect a quarry committee which would negotiate pay and conditions. There was a major strike in 1865 but this was settled, since Lord Penrhyn, while not giving way on the question of a committee or union, met some of the quarrymen's other demands. There were, of course, bad times as well as good. Indeed, emigration from Bethesda to the South Welsh coalfields and to North America started in the 1840's. But on the whole, thanks to rising demand for roofing slates from the rapidly growing industrial cities, the quarries were reasonably prosperous up to about 1880 when the building industry slumped. Production reached its peak at the Penrhyn Quarry as far back as 1862, but on the whole, the period thereafter up to 1880 was reasonably prosperous. However, there was discontent in other quarries and the North Wales Quarrymen's Union was founded in 1874 to strengthen the hand of the quarrymen. Lord Penrhyn himself reacted against demands being made by the quarrymen, and there was a lockout in July 1874 which was settled peaceably through the Pennant-Lloyd Agreement which was regarded as the best possible compromise between the conflicting rights of the workers and those of the employer. This agreement had to be enforced through arbitration, which found for the men.

So, though the 1860's and 1870's were to some extent troubled times in Bethesda, the outlook for industry remained reasonably good. It was not until the 1880's when the building industry stagnated that the Penrhyn Quarry and, indeed, the whole quarrying industry in North Wales began its long decline. In spite of some revival of demand for slates in the 1890's and again after the First World War, there was increasing competition both from imported tiles which were cheaper than slates, and from cheap slates from the United States, France and Portugal. Over the next 100 years there was very little let up in this decline, which has resulted in the closing of all opencast quarries except Penrhyn, where now no more than 300 men are employed as against 3,000 at the peak of production. Otherwise, only two slate mines continue in production at Blaenau Ffestiniog and to do so have to rely to a large extent on tourist visits.

For the quarrymen living in Nant Ffrancon and Bethesda the economic climate became much worse in 1885 when the Hon. G.S. Douglas Pennant took over from his 85 year old father, whom he succeeded the following year as the second Lord Penrhyn. He appointed E.A. Young, a London accountant, intent on applying business principles, as his manager. Douglas Pennant and Young claimed complete freedom to manage the quarry as they thought fit and would not recognise the quarrymen's committee. They wanted the quarry to be run as far as possible like a factory. Young soon abrogated the important Lloyd-Pennant Agreement of 1875 and tried to end the system by which groups of men could bargain for blocks of work.

For their part, the men had always looked upon the quarry as a place to provide work where in due course their sons would be taken on. They were skilled men who considered they should be left some latitude in their working hours, holidays and working methods. The English manager, in their view, knew nothing about slate quarrying. They wanted to be treated humanely as individuals. They did not question the rights of Lord Penrhyn as owner, but they did question his right to dictate working methods.

E.A. Young could not understand the quarrymen: "the more I try and introduce business principles the more they rebel". He thought the Welsh quarrymen "childish and ignorant, easily irritated and making poor foreman material". He instituted heavy fines for those arriving even a little late for work and tried to cut down the traditional holidays. There was bound to be trouble.

THE 1896–97 LOCKOUT AND THE GREAT LOCKOUT OF 1900–1903

The first lockout was in a sense a dress rehearsal for the second, much longer, one. Both were triggered off by the intransigent Lord Penrhyn in the face of the demand from the men to have the right to combine and to negotiate higher wages. In the face of a threat to strike early in the following year, Lord Penrhyn in effect closed the quarries in October 1896. Although the North Wales Quarrymen's Union had very little money to support their members in Bethesda, a great deal of support came from other areas and from other unions. Choirs from Bethesda raised £2,400 and a total of £19.000 was collected all over Britain to sustain the struggle in Bethesda. The effects of the lockout were eased by the fact that more than half the quarrymen were able to get jobs either in neighbouring quarries or in coalmines, docks and brickworks throughout Wales and the North West of England. Others worked on the construction of the Snowdon Mountain Railway. Some emigrated to Western Australia and South Africa.

No one expected an early end to the lockout, but it did, in fact, come within eleven months and then on terms which were, in effect, a victory for Lord Penrhyn. So the smouldering resentment went on and broke out again in 1900. This time the lockout lasted for three whole years; again Bethesda became headline news and the lockout ranked in importance with the war in South Africa. Soon after the lockout started, George Cadbury, the Quaker philanthropist and owner of Bournville Chocolates as well as the Daily News, swung his paper behind the quarrymen and raised over £3,000 on their behalf. Altogether, the quarrymen were able to collect over £41,000 from other unions and connections throughout the country, and a further £32,000 was raised by three choirs, made up of all religious denominations in Bethesda, touring the country.

As time went on, Lord Penrhyn tried from time to time to open the quarries by offering to take men back on his terms. He got a number of men to come and work but few skilled quarrymen. Violent feeling, however, developed between the striking and non-striking quarrymen in Bethesda and, just as in the 1984-5 miners' strike, there were considerable complaints from the local authority about the cost of policing. There were 125 prosecutions for attacks on working quarrymen but only 71 convictions. Normally, there were only five policemen in Bethesda. In this troubled time the numbers were increased to twenty to thirty permanently in the town, with extra police from other authorities and even troops at crisis times. Again, there were complaints about police cruelty and want of tact.

In spite of the efforts of the Board of Trade to get Lord Penrhyn to go to arbitration, he refused and towards the third year of the lockout the trickle of men returning to work increased. But the men who returned to work came overwhelmingly from the villages of Tregarth and Sling below

Bethesda, or from those who had been forced to go and live in Bangor. Quarrymen in Bethesda, and in the northern end of Nant Ffrancon, remained solid in support of the strike.

The strike finally had to come to an end after 3 years, and indeed it did so again more or less on Lord Penrhyn's terms. He and Young were determined to re-fashion their workforce and ensure that only workmen who were "loyal" should be taken on. Black lists had been compiled throughout the 3 years indicating the degree of loyalty or disloyalty, not only of quarrymen but of tenants of farm cottages.

THE EFFECTS OF THE LOCKOUT

Bethesda which had once been a prosperous town with its own vigorous social, cultural and religious life presented a pitiful spectacle after the surrender to Lord Penrhyn's implacable demands and his opposition to any effective form of organisation among the quarrymen. Of the 2,800 men who were employed in the quarry in 1900 fully 1,200 had not been taken back by May 1904. Many emigrated to South Wales or the United States, or even to Patagonia in the Argentine. I have been told that in the Chubut valley, where the Welsh first settled in Patagonia, there is a Bethesda and a group of farms called Maes Caradoc, Pentre and Blaen-y-nant. The emigrants were homesick for Nant Ffrancon. The population of Bethesda fell markedly and membership of the chapels fell too and remained much lower than before the lockout. In spite of the great religious revival of 1905 which was sweeping thousands of hitherto indifferent people into the chapels throughout Wales, the public life of Bethesda became a feeble caricature of what it had been. There was a lack of confidence and Bethesda became a far more depressed place than other quarrying towns and villages in North Wales hit by the decline of the slate industry. Bitterness remained between the families of the striking and working quarrymen which lasted for more than one generation.

RELATIONS BETWEEN THE PENRHYNS, THE QUARRYMEN AND THE FARMERS

In the second half of the 19th century the Penrhyns were, on

Tai Newyddion, Nant Ffrancon about 1890
The two small cottages with turf roofs have disappeared.
(Photo by Gwynfryn Owen, Sling)

the whole, paternal despots wishing to be good landlords and ready to give money for quarrymen's hospitals, houses and welfare. But they were totally unwilling to surrender power, whether in the running of their quarries and farms or politically in holding on to the Caernarfonshire County seat in parliament up to 1880. Their charitable acts did them little good with the quarrymen who kept saying they would prefer to have higher wages than free hospitals.

There was a Royal Commission on Land in Wales in 1893 at which the agent of the Penrhyn estate, Colonel the Hon. William Sackville-West, gave evidence. He maintained that, though most farms were on yearly tenancies, in fact the farmers had their security while being free to quit. He also produced evidence to show that the cottages on the Penrhyn estate, which were mostly occupied by quarrymen, had been built about 1830-40 but that some were being reconstructed in the 1890's. The Commission's Report criticised cottages in Anglesey for having no proper separate bedrooms and having no floors and no privy, which was very much the same as in other parts of Wales, but the cottages on the Penrhyn estate were of a considerably higher standard. Colonel Sackville-West, however, agreed that his inability to talk Welsh, the same inability applying both to agents and landlords generally in North Wales, was to some extent a handicap. He said, "It is, of course, desirable that landowners and their agents should be able to converse with their tenants, but it is to be hoped that as the knowledge of English increases, the inconvenience won't exist and will be gradually abated". In other words, he was assuming that the Welsh farmers would learn English rather than the Penrhyns and their agents would learn Welsh. He confirmed that all tenancy agreements were in English only.

This division in language between farmers, quarrymen and the Penrhyns made it extremely important who did the interpretation at meetings between the two sides in the quarry and in awarding tenancies. There were often disputes as to whether the man chosen was a good interpreter.

In Bethesda in 1901, according to the census returns, a large majority of males could talk Welsh only, although the number who could claim command of both English and Welsh was increasing, probably because it was a good mark to be able to talk both languages. There were only twelve men in Bethesda who said they could only talk English. In Nant Ffrancon at that time there would have been only Welsh speakers and, indeed, to this day people living in Nant Ffrancon are still almost entirely Welsh speakers though, of course, nowadays all except young children are bilingual. The children are brought up in Welsh and learn their English at school. There are exceptions in the children of English people coming to live in Nant Ffrancon who have to learn their Welsh at school. In these cases the children become bilingual, but the parents remain English speaking only unless they learn Welsh at an evening school or on an Ulpan course.

A further division between landlord and tenant was that presented by religion. Bethesda and Nant Ffrancon were overwhelmingly chapel-going; the Penrhyns were Church of England. Within three miles of the centre of Bethesda, including the lower half of Nant Ffrancon, there were by 1870 twenty-nine places of worship, twenty-two of them non-conformist. There were 1,500 more seats in chapels than needed to accommodate the total population of the town. In December 1872, 4,000 people attended non-conformist chapels on Sunday evenings; only 500 went to Church of England churches, The timetable of the chapel-goers on a Sunday was rigorous. For instance, in 1900 at the Jerusalem Methodist Chapel in Bethesda it was as follows:-

9 a.m. prayer meeting for the youth, 10 a.m. sermon, 2 p.m. Sunday School, 5 p.m. singing meeting, 6 p.m. sermon. There were also prayer meetings or Band of Hope classes every weekday evening.

The Church of England in Wales was divided deeply by the argument about disestablishment. Welsh speaking church-goers were strongly in favour of disestablishment, which finally came in 1920. As was to be expected, the Penrhyns and their friends opposed disestablishment.

These divisions went back to an earlier part of the 19th century. The 1847 Report on Education in North Wales brings out very clearly that the standard of teaching in the National and British schools, being in English, was very low. Thanks to the Penrhyns there were two schools in Llandegai village and one at Tyn Tŵr. At the latter school there were 180 boys and girls but only 3 able to read and write well. None were able to recite the catechism. They were ignorant of scripture and geography. The schoolmaster himself was of poor quality. At Llanllechid there was a church school, but the buildings were bad, the Commissioners were particularly scandalised by the lack of lavatories which they maintained led to the children "learning immorality". But the Commissioners were even more impressed with the difficulties of Welsh speaking children. No attempt was made for the transition from Welsh to English through grammars in English and Welsh. The Commissioners reported "that it is difficult to conceive an employment more discouraging than that of the scholars, compelled as they are to employ six hours daily in reading the reciting chapters and formulae in a tongue they cannot understand which neither their books nor their teachers can explain". This was not surprising since the teachers themselves often did not know English.

The 1847 Report on Education in North Wales presents a different picture of the chapel Sunday Schools where the teaching was in Welsh. The product of the Sunday schools was "far superior to the same class of Englishman in being able to read the bible in their own language. Supplied with a variety of religious and poetical literature, and skilled in discussing with eloquence and subtlety, abstruse points of polemic theology, they remain superior in every brand of practical knowledge and skill. Their schools, literature and religious pursuits may have cultivated talents for preaching and poetry but for every other calling they are incapacitated. For secular subjects they have neither literature nor language. In Welsh, although they speak correctly, they can neither write nor spell. They are compelled to employ two languages, one for religion and domestic intercourse, another for the market, in the Courts of Justice, at the Board of Guardians and for the transaction of every other public function and to increase their difficulties the latter language (English) remains, and must continue, an unknown tongue".

"The most ignorant class of people in the County (this is still 1847), are the small farmers. Many do not know the alphabet. They who can read only have the bible and some almanacs in their cottages. Periodicals are read by the quarrymen and tradesmen but not by the farmer. They read nothing. But most quarrymen can only read Welsh." The Report went on to say that the cottages were often squalid huts. The inhabitants had means to live better having peat, wood, bacon, salmon and game but prefer from ignorance to live in squalor. Overcrowding in the cottages was bad for morals and the worst depravity was to be found in quarrying areas. There was not so much serious crime as in England but more illegitimate children. There was no sedition (chartism) in Caernarfonshire. But there was much "unchaste courting in bed".

DISPUTE OVER CROWN LANDS

It was common belief that the Penrhyns had no right to quarry part of the Penrhyn Quarries or to hold the mountain land above and to the west of the quarry. There had been a Crown grant of this land in the form of a lease depending on three lives, the last dying in 1860, which was alleged to have been obtained in 1784 in shady circumstances. Doubts about the claim of the Penrhyn family to this valuable land and some other land above Bethesda, which was also quarried, were voiced in

1849 and again later in the century but no satisfactory reply to complaints was ever received from the Commissioners of Crown Lands and this was the case even when Lloyd George became Chancellor of the Exchequer in 1908. But the war intervened and the Liberals, who were the party keen on land reform, became a dwindling force. The last occasion the issue seems to have been raised was in 1938, but again nothing was settled. It was always an important issue, not only because of the great wealth to be obtained from quarries, but from the rights of cottagers to build their own cottages and have security of tenure. This did not affect the people living in Nant Ffrancon since there was no doubt that the land there belonged to the Penrhyns. But it did affect anybody wishing to build a cottage high on the mountain, either near the Penrhyn Quarry or above Bethesda.

CHAPTER 7

The Present Century

There has been little change this century in the outward beauty of the valley. The mountains have not changed, apart from some landslips, none of which have been catastrophic and the river still follows its old course, even though its bed has been lowered. The biggest outward change has been the transformation of Tyn-y-maes from being a quarrymen's village of at least 100 inhabitants with two chapels and a shop, into its present shrunken condition of a motel and half a dozen houses. The other main change has been the enormous increase of traffic along the A5. This has led to the widening of the road, especially along the south side of Llyn Ogwen, so that the road now takes the heaviest lorries as well as, in the summer, a constant stream of cars and caravans where only eighty five years ago there was an occasional horse-drawn vehicle. The old road on the west of the valley has been metalled and tarred, so it is no longer the rutted and grassy track it used to be. Cattle grids have replaced gates, and there are many more tourist cars as well as farmers' landrovers.

For the past thirty years the peace of the valley has been shattered several times a day in most months by pairs of jet fighters screaming down the valley practising low flying tactics. The aircraft come in from the south-east flying at about 300 feet above Llyn Ogwen, bank sharply to the right down Nant Ffrancon and then climb steeply over Bethesda. The sheep and cattle pay no attention, but human conversation has to stop.

In spite of a great increase in walkers and climbers, there are the same mountain paths, but some of them have had to be rebuilt because of the erosion caused by the tramp of so many feet. So they stand out more in the landscape.

The only new buildings are mountain huts such as those of the Scouts and climbing clubs, and the extensions both to Idwal Youth Hostel and the large addition by Birmingham Education Authority to Ogwen Cottage. Farm buildings have not changed except for a big new barn at Tyn-y-maes and some outbuildings falling into disrepair at farms which have been run together.

As in many other parts of the country, the Second War stimulated new activity in the valley. In 1940 fears of invasion led to tank traps and pill boxes being built to deny an invader the use of both the A5 and the old road. Ogwen became a centre for mountain warfare training. Evacuees from bombed Liverpool and London came to occupy some cottages, but drifted back home by 1941. At Maes Caradoc there were German Jewish refugees, mainly women and children whose menfolk had been interned on the Isle of Man. One boy, only fifteen at the time, lived contentedly, alone, at Maes Caradoc cottage for several months. He recorded in his letters to his parents in an Isle of Man internment camp his great satisfaction at being able to work for his preliminary medical exams in the peace and quiet of Nant Ffrancon and how Mr. & Mrs. John Jones at Maes Caradoc farm took great interest in him, providing milk and butter and, as he was to study medicine, getting him to help at the birth of a calf. He used to play Haydn, Bach, Mozart and Handel on his violin, sometimes out of doors. He wrote that leaving Maes Caradoc was out of the question because "nowhere would I find so much peace". Even an earthquake on 12th December 1940 failed to disturb him. (The Ogwen Valley like most of Caernarfonshire is liable to earthquakes. There was quite a noisy one as recently as July 1984).

The agricultural subsidies introduced just before the war, and extended during the war, led Mr. Jones and the other farmers in the valley to increase production considerably. In spite of all the wartime transport difficulties the quarries, too, had more work in providing slates for war damaged roofs in the big cities.

The bed of the Ogwen River was lowered expensively in the late 1960s with the help of huge crawler excavators, so as to try and drain the marshy ground which for centuries has occupied more than half the valley floor. The river banks, as a result of being covered with excavated stones, have not yet regained their beautiful turf and there are less birds breeding there. Indeed, the whooper swans have totally disappeared. In spite of the lowering of the river bed the marshes still persist, but at least the valley is no longer flooded after heavy rainfall.

Ogwen Bridge
Etching by David Woodford.

106

A pipeline was built in 1974 from Ffynnon Llugwy down the valley to provide the villages round Tregarth and, indeed, Bangor itself, with the water which used to come from Llyn Marchlyn before it became the upper lake for the Dinorwig electricity pump storage system. The pipeline is buried and its route hardly shows now, but it caused the destruction of some fine oak trees below Tyn-y-maes. There has, until recently, been a greater threat from Bangor's forecast future demands for water, which would have entailed taking water out of Llyn Cowlyd and building a small reservoir and purification plant at Ceunant at the bottom of Nant Ffrancon. The Welsh Water Authority also planned a new road from Tyn-y-maes to carry heavy vehicles across a concrete bridge over the Ogwen River to build and maintain the works. In April 1986, however, the Authority decided to postpone the scheme for the time being because demand for water (presumably thanks to declining manufacturing industry) was not then expected to grow as had been anticipated.

Although outwardly the valley does not seem to have changed much since the beginning of the century, the number and way of life of the people living there has changed markedly. It is true that nearly everyone living in the valley is Welsh speaking and the farmers still tend their sheep in the traditional manner, but the occupation of most inhabitants is likely to be concerned with conservation or with mountaineering rather than with sheep farming. Together, the National Trust, the Youth Hostel Association, Mountain Training Centres, the Scouts, the Nature Conservancy Council and the Snowdonia National Park Authority provide more jobs than does sheep farming. The number of sheep in the valley has risen steeply, but the number of farmers and shepherds has at least halved. All the quarrymen and their families have gone.

The farmers continue to have a hard life, dominated by following traditional methods of sheep farming and by the vagaries of the climate, especially the heavy rainfall. A big change might have come when the Penrhyn Estate sold its mountain land and farms in 1951. At that time only the farmers at the lower end of Nant Ffrancon bought their farms after they and their predecessors had for 500 years been tenants of the Penrhyn family and their predecessors. The National Trust acquired through the Treasury all the rest of the land in the valley and, indeed, extended their holding in 1984. So now all but two farms in the valley are occupied by tenants of the National Trust. The new landlord has a policy, in so far as its resources allow, of improving farm houses and buildings (mostly built in the 19th century) and of repairing stone walls and planting trees. So there has not yet been any change in the farming landscape which the Trust wishes to conserve.

Although life is still hard for the sheep farmer, it has been made much more secure by subsidies, now mainly from the Common Market, which in many years provides most of the farmers' net income. As a result, the farmers can now afford a land rover and a tractor instead of relying on a welsh cob, and their houses are much more comfortable, especially since the arrival of mains electricity in 1972. Electricity, too, has made shearing easier, as machines have replaced hand shears. The double deck trailers drawn by land rovers, owned by most farmers, make them more independent in transporting sheep. It is only occasionally one sees flocks of sheep on the roads. But there are no shops, schools or chapels in the valley and no buses along the A5 as before the war. So shopping or chapel-going means driving to Bethesda. School children are taken to Bethesda by taxi. With the closing of the branch railway line to Bethesda in 1963 the nearest railway station is at Bangor.

Thanks to subsidies and the additional income which can be earned from holidaymakers, there is now some sort of stability in the valley, though it is dependent on sufficient farming families being prepared to earn their main livelihood on the rain swept mountains. It has also only been made possible by the amalgamation of farms, so that some of the farms are now worked from a distance. Anyone working in the valley today is bound to ask himself whether the present rather uneasy balance could be maintained if subsidies were abolished or even drastically reduced.

Farmers with long memories are convinced that the land is not so well farmed as it was at the beginning of the century if only because there are far fewer people working on the land. Farms are now run either by the family without the help of agricultural labourers or are farmed at a distance from some lowland base. Although good transport and mains electricity have increased productivity there is not enough labour to clear bracken, mend walls and clear out drains. So the bracken has spread on the mountain slopes, the walls have decayed and some drains are blocked. If the National Trust can carry out its improvement schemes standards of farming should rise, but at best it will be a slow process.

Another change that strikes visitors is that farmers' wives no longer sell their own eggs, milk and butter, so to that extent they have become less independent. Most of the farmhouses now have only traces of the water wheels which used to power the butter churns with water from the mountain streams. Only a few farms have hens scratching round the farmhouse, and the milk produced is strictly for the calves.

CHANGES BELOW THE VALLEY

The biggest change this century has been the decline of the Penrhyn slate quarries and the closing of other much smaller quarries, such as Moel Faban and Coetmor above Bethesda. Employment before the lockout in 1900 in Penrhyn was nearly 3000 men. By 1914 it was under 2000, by 1946 about 1000 and now 300, a slight improvement over a nadir of 250 men in 1972. As a result, Bethesda has been a depressed area throughout this century, except for some revival after both wars. Its population has fallen from about 6000 to 4000 and if it has now reached some sort of equilibrium at a fairly low level of activity, this has been due to the introduction of light industry, to money spent in the shops by tourists, to the buying up of quarrymen's cottages as second homes and to its becoming, to some extent, a dormitory town for people working in Bangor. Although those with John Betjeman's architectural tastes can find some pleasure in the facades of the enormous 19th century chapels and in the removal of the slate tips from the middle of the town, I still find the main street rather sad.

Things may improve when eventually the A5 bypass is built, so that the summer traffic jams no longer block Bethesda's streets. The rebuilding of the A55 along the north coast should also help to cut down the number of very heavy lorries using the A5. At present, these heavy lorries do not use the A55 because they cannot pass the low gateway through Conwy's medieval walls.

Penrhyn Quarry
Moel Faban and Cwm Caseg in the background.
Photo by Steve Ashton.

111

THE PENRHYN QUARRY

The Great Pit with its tiers of working galleries, dug out over the last two centuries is still an awe inspiring sight, especially when seen from above. The old tramways for bringing up the slate rock have been replaced by roads, along which huge dumper trucks grind with their heavy loads. The quarry no longer belongs to the Penrhyn family, having been bought by Sir Alfred MacAlpine Limited in 1964. But it is still possible to see the old *cabans,* in which the Penrhyn workers had their midday meetings to work out ways of getting better conditions from their Penrhyn employers in the 19th century — as well as to sing, recite poetry and play word games.

At present, most of the quarry's earnings come from roofing slate, but such production only employs 125 out of a total of over 300 employees, even though much of the splitting of slate is still done by hand. There is now an architectural slate department, where slabs of fine slate are carved to form features such as floors or plaques in new public buildings. A great effort, too, has been made to profit from the huge waste tips which have built up over the last 200 years to provide fill for road schemes such as the Bangor bypass and for Fullersite slate dust, which is used in a variety of products from bricks to toothpaste. There is also much quarrying for roadstone. Huge lorries come to take the stone all over the country, but with high transport costs the company find it difficult to compete with the established roadstone quarries, such as Penmaenmawr.

Half the present workforce in the quarry comes from Bethesda. Most of the rest used to work at Dinorwig quarry before it closed in 1969 or are drawn from a 10 mile radius. During the long decline of the quarry, the trade of a quarryman lost its earlier prestige. In the 19th century it was the ambition of most schoolboys to follow their father into the quarry. In the state of low morale that prevailed the 1900-1903 lockout a quarryman's job was less well regarded. But now it is certainly no longer looked down on and turnover of labour at the quarry is low.

The Penrhyn family power was bound to diminish with the decline of quarrying and with the agricultural slump between the wars. As has been mentioned, after the Second World War 40,000 acres of Penrhyn land passed to the National Trust and the quarry was run down to 300 men.

The radical Liberal Welsh middle class were never able to replace the Penrhyns as the wielders of economic power. In the local economy the Penrhyns' power was not taken over; rather it disintegrated. Looking at the area of the old Penrhyn estates, it is difficult to say who are the people with most power and influence now. Certainly the farmers have some claim to this position, given their greater prosperity through subsidies. But many are small men and farm their farms as family units. The Welsh Department of Agriculture, the Welsh Water Authority and the Electricity Generating Board have great influence on Nant Ffrancon and surrounding country. But their power in a mixed economy is very different from that of the Penrhyns. It is modified by the various pressure groups, both local and national, such as the National Trust, the Countryside Commission, the Snowdonia National Park Society, the Nature Conservancy Council and the Council for the Protection of Rural Wales.

As the economy more and more depends on holidaymakers, those who provide holidays and those who benefit from the new trades are likely to have a greater say in what is done. There is some new industry in Bethesda, but not enough. There are still plenty of empty factories and many shops in the main street are closed. That Bethesda still has a population of about 4,000 is due, in different degrees, to the Welfare State which enables people to stay there through social security payments, to the growing holiday trade and to the prosperity of the farming community and of neighbouring Bangor.

I have sketched briefly the main changes that have taken place in the valley this century, and which have produced a rather uneasy balance in the way of life of its inhabitants. There are three main intertwining strands which are of special interest, both in themselves and because they are likely to determine the future. They are also the main activities in the valley — sheep farming, mountaineering and conservation.

CHAPTER 8
Sheep Farming

The sheep farmers in the valley still follow the same round of the year as in the previous century. The breeding ewes are brought down from the mountain in March and lambing starts in early April, in spite of the often very severe weather. Just after lambing starts the previous year's ewe lambs come back from the lowland farms where they have been wintering and are sent up the mountain, even though the spring grass has not yet begun to grow. Few ewes have twin lambs, but even to feed one lamb is difficult for some.

A few lambs have to be bottle fed. In spite of the farmer and his wife working round the clock, the cold wet weather and the foxes take their toll. It will be a good year in which eighty-five lambs survive for every one hundred ewes.

By May, once the grass does start growing, most of the flock moves up the mountain above the fence which marks the upper limit of the ffridd, the main enclosed grazing area just above the farm. There is by now more grass on the mountain than in the valley which has been grazed bare by the lambing ewes. The sooner the lambs get to know their flocks' territory (the *cynefin*) the better, as they will be unlikely to stray later onto neighbouring farms whose land also extends up onto the open mountain. A strong inherited instinct built up over the generations keeps the flock on its territory and thus makes shepherding easier. Hence a flock is normally sold with the farm it grew up on and as such commands a higher price.

Only the ewes with wether lambs (castrated ram lambs) soon to be sold, stay below the fence mainly on the meadows on the valley floor, which are not reserved for hay or silage. Nowadays, farmers often do not make hay or silage. In their view, it is not worthwhile since the summer rains often lead to the hay being spoilt. This, of course, would not apply to silage, but silage can often be difficult to make and maintain in good condition. So it may be cheaper to buy in any winter feed needed and use all the meadows for fattening lambs.

The flock is rounded up, usually in June, for the first of two compulsory dips against scab, and again at the beginning of July

Sheep shearing at Maes Caradoc in the 1930's.

for shearing, which used to be done by hand, the sheep with their legs tied together being laid on wooden benches. To shear a sheep in four minutes was good going. Now electricity is used and the shearing goes quicker. Both the rounding up of the sheep and the shearing are still co-operative activities in which neighbouring farms join forces, the gathering and shearing days of each farm being staggered so that enough manpower is available for each in turn. Several men and their dogs are needed to gather a flock and to shear it quickly before the weather changes. It is wasteful to shear in wet weather. Fleeces heat up and go mouldy if rolled up and stored wet. Although thanks to electric shears, farmers do some of their shearing in small batches there is also a main shearing day at which a generous mid-day dinner is provided in the farmhouse. The harvest is made up of the neatly rolled fleeces stacked in the barn awaiting the wool merchant to come and buy. The sheep used to be washed before shearing, but this is not now considered necessary.

In September, the wether lambs and those ewe lambs which are not destined to join the breeding flock are sent to market, either to the butcher or for fattening. At the end of October the rest of the ewe lambs go down to the lowlands for the winter. Before this these ewe lambs have been separated from their mothers to give the ewes a chance of putting on weight before they face the winter on the mountain. The tupping season for the dozen or so mature rams on the farm is in November when they are released to mate with the ewes which have been brought down below the fence. Some of the rams will have been bought at other farms to lessen in-breeding in the flock and cannot be allowed onto the open mountains, as they might wander and serve ewes on neighbouring farms. A good ram will serve at least fifty ewes.

After tupping most of the flock goes up the mountain again only being brought down if there is too much snow. Wherever they are they continue to graze on whatever grass they can find, only being fed hay or cake in exceptional circumstances, such as the mountains being under snow for a long period. The most they usually get, except at lambing time, is a concentrated block of molasses, urea and other proteins which they can lick. To the layman it is astonishing how a ewe on such a low winter diet can give birth to her lambs and give suck, especially where there are twins. Not surprisingly, breeding ewes need a gentler climate after four years on the mountain. So they are sold off to a lowland farm where they are often crossed with a Suffolk ram to produce two more crops of lambs before finally going to the slaughterhouse.

This progression through the year has been followed all through this century. There have been no extensive experiments in the valley in bringing the breeding ewes under cover in the winter and letting them lamb indoors to protect them from the cold and marauding foxes, or of giving the ewes more winter feed than has been judged absolutely necessary in the past. Although work on winter feeding has been going on at at the Agricultural Development and Advisory Service Centre at Pentrefoelas, the general view in the valley seems to be that it pays better to keep the ewes hardy and finding their own food. This is in spite of the A.D.A.S. experiment showing that with more winter feeding the ewes grow bigger and stronger and, by producing more milk, are able to rear bigger and stronger lambs. The Department of Agriculture local animal husbandry officer in Bangor is convinced that Nant Ffrancon could grow enough grass and silage in the summer to provide far more winter food than is at present grown. He argues that the sheep should have even feeding throughout the year, rather than glut in the summer peak and too much scarcity in the winter. But, so far, the farmers in the valley do not seem to have been convinced. They doubt whether they could, in practice, produce the extra feed to nourish the bigger stronger sheep envisaged. Indeed, in recent years the tendency has been not to make the amount of hay and silage that was common in the past. The farmers' reluctance to try new methods may well be due less to conservatism than to doubt whether they would, in fact, pay. There is plenty of awareness of new ideas but the pattern of farming is largely set by the climate and the mountains.

Nevertheless, there has, particularly in the last forty years, been a steady increase in both the number and quality of sheep in the valley. Indeed, in the last ten years sheep numbers have been increasing generally in North Wales at a rate of 2 to 3% per annum and the same is most probably true of the valley. The care and breeding of sheep has also become more scientific thanks to the expert advice provided by A.D.A.S. which has done much to eliminate disease as well as to improve breeding.

The main change in the make up of the flock came after the First World War. Up to then farmers kept a considerable number of wethers on the mountain for four years for the heavier fleeces and the large joints of mutton they provided when sold. Since the 1920s the main market has increasingly been in lamb rather than mutton, so a higher proportion of the flock goes to the butcher each year and the mountain pasture does not get the dunging the wethers provided. Indeed, there have been virtually no wethers on the mountains for the past thirty years. Hence, nowadays there is a greater drain on the minerals in the mountain grass which cannot be compensated for artificially in that most of the pastures are on steep mountain slopes. It is not worth while spreading expensive fertiliser on these slopes only to see it soon washed off by heavy rains, quite apart from the difficulty of transporting fertilisers high up. The most the farmers can do is to lime and slag the meadow fields on the valley floor.

The present (1986) subsidy system (the EEC sheep meat

regime) provides a powerful incentive to keep as many sheep as the pasture allows. This is because there is now, in effect, a subsidy of about £12 per breeding ewe for some farmers. This is made up of a straight headage subsidy which is £6.75 per breeding ewe plus a variable premium on sales of fat lambs which works out at about another £6, but only for those farmers who can fatten their own lambs on a big scale. In the harsh conditions of the upper Ogwen valley this means only those farmers who have lowland farms as well. The others, such as Maes Caradoc, can only fatten a small proportion of the flock.

There has been some controversy about how far this system of subsidy has led to over-stocking in the valley. There seems some evidence that there could be over-stocking on the common land on the Carneddau mountains above Bethesda where the commoners have registered their right to run about 20,000 sheep as well as cattle and mountain ponies, on the 12,000 acres available. In practice, there are far fewer sheep run on the Carneddau; so the danger is more potential than actual. Normally the allowance is more like one sheep to one acre averaged over the year, more in summer, less in winter. It is, of course, very difficult to prevent over-stocking on open mountain where, with pressure of numbers, the sheep will wander off their home territory. The general view in the valley, however, seems to be that over-stocking is self-defeating, since the sheep are then inadequately fed and produce smaller and weaker lambs. Where there is over-stocking, sheep are likely to forage beyond their territory on which they have been brought up and the fact that a fence has recently been built from Nant Peris to the top of Foel Goch shows that there is some concern that this could happen. However, in the opinion of the animal husbandry officer there is already a good check on the numbers of breeding ewes through the subsidy system, since payments are not made beyond the number that a given farm can properly feed. Sheep are counted not only on the mountain farm but also the number of yearlings, that is ewe lambs sent down in the winter, are counted on their winter farms as a check. If the normal ratio of one ewe lamb to three breeding ewes (the number necessary to ensure replacement) is exceeded, then some subsidy may be withheld.

There has been considerable criticism of the subsidy system on the grounds that it has been used too crudely to increase production, while the purpose of the present system in terms of the EEC Policy Directive 75/268 is "To ensure the continuation of farming, thereby maintaining a minimum population level and conserving the countryside". Critics maintain that the scheme has been a very costly way of increasing production and has done so at the expense of both rural communities and the countryside. Money has been wasted by subsiding the most prosperous farmers while denying adequate support for the small (often part-time) farmer for whom it was originally meant. The critics would, however, concede that the system has assisted the preservation of sheep farming and that it has slowed down the decline of the farming population and the rate at which farms are being amalgamated. Nevertheless, it seems clear that it is the big scale farmer who benefits most. The high subsidies on breeding ewes mean that he has a sure base on which he can raise credit for capital improvements which are, to some extent, grant aided though less than in the past.

Even more important, it is normally the bigger farmers with enough feed or lowland meadows to be able to fatten their own lambs who benefit. The small mountain farmer is not able to fatten lambs as he has not got the right sort of pasture.

In Nant Ffrancon most of the farmers have medium size farms, that is up to about 1,000 acres. These farmers have done well enough in that they have been able to continue farming, but the farmers who have done best are two or three others who farm in the lowlands as well as in the Ogwen Valley and on a sufficiently large scale to be able, if they wish, to carry out capital improvements.

There is, therefore, an incentive to amalgamate farms. This has already taken place in Nant Ffrancon to the extent that only three out of the seven farms are inhabited by farming families, a state of affairs similar to that of neighbouring valleys. The pace has quickened in the last ten years and is likely to go further especially if there is any marked reduction in subsidies. This is so although amalgamation of farms often means one farm is run from a distance, and hence more sheep are lost than when the shepherd lives on the spot and sees his flock often. But the short term loss sustained is less than the cost of a shepherd. As against this, over time the farm itself declines as walls, fences, bracken clearing and drainage all suffer.

Hill farm subsidies have succeeded in Nant Ffrancon in stabilising the farming population, admittedly at a very low level, and has ensured that sheep farming continues at a reasonably high standard on the farms that are inhabited and at an acceptable though lower level on the farms run from a distance. But the farmers would be very vulnerable to any marked decrease in subsidy. The National Trust, as a major landlord, might try and offset some of the loss of income to the farmer by reducing rents, but there is clearly not much than can be done in this way, especially if the Trust tried to give equivalent treatment to its other farmers who might be affected by cuts in other subsidies. The National Trust and the Snowdonia National Park Authority would, no doubt, intensify efforts already made, and which are discussed later, to encourage farmers to diversify by supplementing income from small scale forestry or from holidaymakers, but this could hardly offset a marked decline in subsidy.

The upper Ogwen valley, together with its neighbouring valleys, has recently suffered another threat to sheep farming which, conceivably, could recur. This was the Chernobyl nuclear power accident in Russia in April 1986. The valley suffered through heavy rain bringing down radio active fall out, particularly caesium, as the main radiation cloud passed over the mountains. Although tests during the following few months showed widely different readings, some lambs registered up to 2,000 bequerels per kilo. The Ministry of Agriculture imposed restrictions on the movement and marketing of lambs and required that all lambs sent to market should be branded with a bright blue mark on their neck. As the lambs could not be slaughtered it was not surprising that the price fetched at the first sales at the end of August 1986 was less than half that at similar sales the previous year. The Government announced that a fund of £5 million would be available to compensate the North Wales farmers affected, but it was not clear to what extent actual losses would be compensated. There is also the nagging worry that there could be another nuclear accident with similar results. It is ironic that it should be the sheep farmers in remote and peaceful valleys of Snowdonia (as well as those in Cumbria and Scotland) who should be the main sufferers in Britain from the Chernobyl explosion.

CHAPTER 9

Mountaineering and Rock Climbing in the Ogwen Valley

Rock climbing in the Ogwen Valley is rather less than 100 years old, although there was plenty of mountaineering and gully climbing in the previous two centuries.

The Ogwen Valley and the rock faces on Craig yr Ysfa and at the head of the Llafar Valley afford some of the best climbs in Snowdonia. In the Ogwen Valley itself there is a whole string of rock faces from the lesser known climbs on Carnedd y Filiast and Foel Goch to the famous routes in and around the Devil's Kitchen, the Idwal Slabs, both Glyderau, Tryfan, and indeed right up to the slimey rocks of Gallt yr Ogof. There are even good climbs on Craig Braich-ty-du on the slopes of Pen yr Oleu Wen. The number of first ascents of new climbs has varied from year to year in the past, but although the latest (1982) guidebook describes over 420 distinct climbs in the Ogwen Valley alone, no doubt more will be found and conquered in the years to come.

Once North Wales had been opened up to tourists and visitors in the late 18th century, there were growing numbers of people walking to the top of Snowdon by the easiest route and sometimes up the Glyderau as well. Indeed, these two walks became the accepted thing to do for the more energetic, especially if writing a travel book. Some of their achievements were quite considerable, given that the first accurate one inch Ordnance Survey Map did not appear until 1841.

Thomas Pennant described a walk in 1775, that at the time must have seemed very strenuous, from Pen-y-Gwryd along the miners' track over Glyder Fawr, down the Gribin to Llyn Ogwen, then up to Idwal and the Devil's Kitchen and down again past Llyn y Cwn into Nant Peris. It was in 1798 that Rev. W. Bingley describes an ascent of Tryfan from Bochlwyd in which, "We could scarcely take half a dozen steps together in any place without at the same time using our hands". Most travellers had the help of a local guide and were particularly keen to arrive at the summit of their mountain either at sunset or sunrise, so as to

Tryfan in winter.

Y Garn in winter.

record suitable emotions.

With the foundation of the Alpine Club in 1857 these walks and scrambles became more adventurous and, indeed, began to rank as climbs, usually up the larger gullies. Members of the Alpine Club increasingly came to the inn at Pen-y-Gwryd in the 1860s, particularly in the winter, so as to practice for their summer climbs in the Alps. One of them, Charles Matthews, records how in 1861, he failed to "get up from Llyn Idwal to the summit of Glyder Fawr by a beeline". However, Matthews and his friends sometimes used to drive from the railway station at Bangor to Ogwen in a carriage, which then went on to Capel Curig and Pen-y-Gwryd with their luggage, while they climbed over Snowdon and the Glyderau.

In 1870 the Society of Welsh Rabbits was founded at Pen-y-Gwryd. Sometimes members of the Alpine Club brought over their Swiss guides and the standard of climbing, still in gullies on Snowdon and the Devil's Kitchen and Tryfan, began to rise. The first recorded climb away from the gullies and on the mountain face, was Pinnacle Rib on the east face of Tryfan, which was climbed by J.M. Archer Thompson in 1894.

By 1898 the Climber's Club for people devoted to climbing in the British Isles was formed. Its members divided their time in North Wales between the inn at Pen-y-Pass and Ogwen Cottage — then a simple guest house. Leading members of this group were Geoffrey Winthrop Young, J.M. Archer Thompson and W.P. Reade. It was Thompson who first climbed the Devil's Kitchen by cutting steps in the frozen waterfall in 1895, but W.P. Reade did the climb entirely on rock in 1898.

By 1900 these climbers were moving out of their gullies and on to rocks, slabs and faces, using cracks in the rock face for holds, while before they had looked for chimneys which they could ascend by pressure of back and knees. Geoffrey Young's climbing parties came to use the inn at Pen-y-Pass rather than Ogwen Cottage, but would drive round to Ogwen in a smart brake and pair (complete with silver buckles and pipe clay provided by Rawson Owen, a former cavalry four-in-hand whip, and by then landlord at Pen-y-Pass), so that they could climb on the Glyderau and the Carneddau. In the years before the Great War the standard of climbing advanced considerably thanks to such climbers as Siegmund Hertford, Hugh Pope and George Mallory, who died climbing Everest in 1924. The main climbs on

Foel Goch in winter from Pen yr Oleu Wen.

Foel Goch and Elidir in winter.

the Milestone Buttress on the east face of Tryfan and on Glyder Fawr were worked out in this period.

The Direct Route on Glyder Fach was first climbed in 1907 and was then judged to be the hardest climb in North Wales. It now ranks as a "hard severe" — that is only about halfway up the scale of difficulty.

Easier routes on the Idwal Slabs were also explored and the Great Gully on Craig-yr-Ysfa and the Western Gully on Black Ladders in Cwm Llafar became favourite climbs. There were great hopes of good climbing on the Craig Gleision Ridge above Pentre, but these were disappointed. However, so much had been done that J.M. Archer Thompson was able to publish his guidebook to rock climbs in the Ogwen Valley in 1910. This was the first of a whole succession of guidebooks, revised about every ten or fifteen years, in which the climbs are named and recorded in the approved manner by the Climber's Club. Between the wars, Geoffrey Young who had lost a leg on the Italian Front in the First War, still ran his Easter climbing parties at Pen-y-Pass. The more energetic members pioneered new routes in the Ogwen Valley as well as on Lliwedd and on Clogwyn Du'r Arddu. The steeper, more exposed rock faces were explored as balance techniques of climbing improved. Geoffrey Young would stump up to Idwal on his peg leg to give advice to beginners struggling up the slabs. He had in the 1920s climbed major peaks in the Alps, including the Matterhorn, using the same peg leg. To compensate for his much slower speed approaching the climb he would keep going through the night while the rest of his party slept in a mountain hut.

At first, most rock climbers, especially those at Pen-y-Pass were drawn mainly from the professional upper middle classes. They were dons or undergraduates from Oxford and Cambridge, successful lawyers, schoolmasters and politicians, who had the time and money for holidays in North Wales as well as in the Alps. They achieved much in the Ogwen Valley, especially in the period 1925-1939 when they shared their successes with new young climbers from Liverpool and from Bangor, most of whom had a very different social background and an even greater determination to excel. It was in this period that the opening of mountain huts at Helyg by the Climber's Club in 1925, at Tal-y-braich by the Rambler's Association in 1927 and the Idwal Youth Hostel in 1932, meant that many more climbers with little

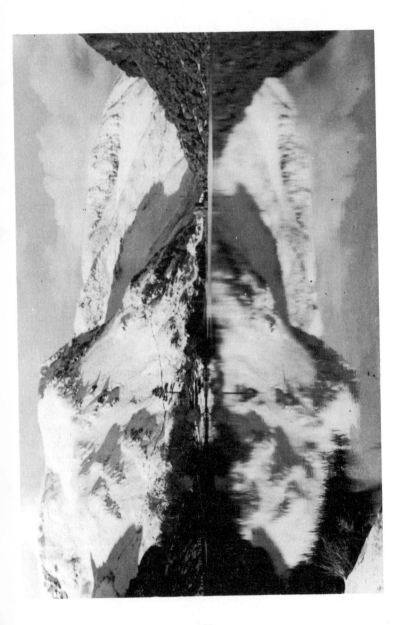

money were able to come to the mountains throughout the year. The advent of the mass produced motor car helped too.

Typical of the Pen-y-Pass climbers were Noel Odell, of Everest fame, who was to pioneer the Tennis Shoe route on Idwal Slabs, as well as the Holly Tree Wall, Jack Longland who achieved the extremely difficult Javelin Blade climb on the Idwal Slabs and Gino Watkins, all of whom were first rate mountaineers as well as rock climbers. Of the same type, but not from the Pen-y-Pass party, as his family had the cottage at Maes Caradoc, was Ted Hicks. A man of great strength and exceptionally long arms, Hicks was the first to do direct starts on Terrace Wall Variant on Tryfan in 1928 and soon after a direct start of the Holly Tree Wall climb, as well as the extremely difficult Rowan Tree Slabs at Idwal. His girdle traverse of Holly Tree Wall was also a remarkable achievement. Among the women climbers George Mallory's daughters, Clare and Berridge, were outstanding.

Typical of local Bangor climbers were E. Pentir Williams, I. ap G. Hughes and Scotty Dwyer, who became a professional climber and was closely associated with the Idwal Youth Hostel. In particular, they pioneered the Great Central Route on Llech Du in Cwm Llafar. The really outstanding climbers of the 1930s were A.B. Hargreaves, J. Menlove Edwards and Colin Kirkus, all from Liverpool or the North of England, though they climbed a good deal with a group of climbers from Cambridge. Edwards founded Liverpool University Rock Climbing Club in 1930 and used the Helyg hut as his base, from which he climbed mainly in the Ogwen district. In particular, he did new climbs near the Devil's Kitchen, on the Milestone Buttress and on Terrace Wall on Tryfan, and on Gallt yr Ogof above Helyg which hardly anyone else visited. He later climbed a lot with an outstanding young Cambridge climber, Wilfred Noyce on Tryfan, Glyder Fawr and on the major new climbs then being worked out on Lliwedd and Clogwyn Du'r Arddu. Together they wrote the 1937 guidebook to Tryfan, Edwards having previously produced his Cwm Idwal guide.

Foel Goch and Llyn Ogwen
(Snowdonia National Park Authority Photo)

The real explosion in rock climbing came after the Second World War, perhaps because the impetus gained in the 1930s was carried on during the war by those in charge of mountain warfare training. After the fiasco of the Norwegian campaign of 1940, great attention was paid to really tough training to ensure that there were enough troops skilled in climbing and skiing to fight any campaign if, for instance, part of the Second Front was to be in Norway. Indeed, a whole division, the 52nd (Scottish Lowland) Division was trained for mountain warfare. In the event, the Division's first battle was on the flooded island of Walcheren in an attempt to take Antwerp in September 1944.

Ogwen became a centre for army mountain training with live ammunition being fired on some mountains. Not only were pill boxes and machine guns built to oppose any German invasion in 1940, but the Idwal Slabs in Tryfan were festooned with ropes of soldiers learning the elements of rock climbing. Their instructors reached an extraordinary high standard of physical fitness with the result that in 1945 one of them, C. Preston, climbed Suicide Wall in Cwm Idwal, which even Hicks and Edwards had found unclimbable.

But it was not just that many soldiers had learned to rock climb that led after the war to the Ogwen Valley becoming more and more attractive to rock climbers. Full employment, paid holidays, cheaper motoring (once petrol rationing had been lifted) and a widespread interest in mountaineering, culminating in the news of the conquest of Everest on Coronation Day in 1953, led to an influx of climbers to North Wales. More huts were opened in the Ogwen Valley. University College of London had a hut at Gwern-y-gof Isaf, the Midlands Association of Mountaineers bought a large wooden bungalow at the end of Llyn Ogwen, which has since been rebuilt. The Climber's Club — now with over six hundred members — acquired two additional huts in the Llanberis Pass in addition to Helyg, which was made more comfortable. An extension was built to Idwal Youth Hostel which also took over the little school building of the 1880s, which looks like a chapel. Ogwen Cottage, bought by Birmingham Education Authority and greatly extended with a large 'building splendid for housing students and teaching mountain skills but quite out of scale with the original cottage,

Carreg Cannau with Penrhyn Quarry.
(Photo·by Martin W. Roberts)

129

added to the accommodation available. In 1984 the car park at Idwal was tidied up and, perhaps sadly, the tea shack, which flourished for so many years by the bridge over the Ogwen Falls, was rehoused in a solid slate building in the same style as the adjoining public lavatories. The Scouts did well too in having a stone hut built at considerable expense in 1960 on the old road leading down to Nant Ffrancon. The planners required that it should look like a cow shed. So normal size windows, which would have allowed the Scouts to look across to the head of Nant Ffrancon, were forbidden; hence the narrow slit windows, high up, to allow some light in but too high to see the magnificent view. Down Nant Ffrancon the Admiralty bought the cottage at Tai Newyddion for mountain training, and reconstructed the interior to allow large parties of naval ratings or WRNS. The officer in charge was quartered in a smart little hut at the back. With the coming of electricity in 1972, these and other mountain huts, such as the two converted farm barns at Pentre, became more comfortable.

In addition to these new permanent huts and hostels for climbers and walkers, improvement in lightweight camping equipment after the war, and the usual shortage of money among the young, led to widespread camping in the valley. Before the war anyone who camped, especially at Easter, was regarded as being very tough and adventurous. But after the war, more and more tents appeared, especially at weekends, at the head of Nant Ffrancon, round Idwal and even at Bochlwyd. Later the Nature Conservancy Council and the National Trust tried to discourage camping where there was a threat to the environment, but the wardens have always been tolerant of the careful camper. Moreover, the campsite at Gwern-y-gof Isaf provides space for more than one hundred tents and caravans.

It was not only camping equipment that became lighter and more weatherproof. Climbing equipment too was transformed after the war. Heavy leather climbing boots, nailed first with hobnails, then clinkers and finally, in the 1930s, with saw-toothed tricounis, gave way to lighter boots and rubber vibram sols. Rubber soled gym shoes, or just socks, had been used for particularly difficult climbs before the war, but the vibram sole gave a good grip on both rock and steep mountain slopes. They were only inferior to nailed boots on wet, slimy rocks or on frozen snow.

Light nylon rope replaced heavy hemp rope which doubled its weight when wet. But care has to be taken with nylon which melts with the friction of another rope running across it. However, nylon is ideal for long pitches when the amount of rope which the leader takes out from his second supporting climber may be as long as 200 feet, and for loops, each fitted with a snap link or karabiner, which enables the leader to protect himself from falling far by hooking the loops over spikes of rock.

Heavy tweed jackets which got soaked with rain were replaced by the lighter grenfell cloth wind jacket, which was only partially rainproof. Later still, light rainproof nylon and other artificial fibres such as Gore-tex came in which meant that it was possibly to stay almost dry in a Welsh downpour, using light and highly portable garments.

Thanks to the use of this new equipment and to the practice of hammering in pitons, which was frowned upon before the war, the standard of climbs achieved has gone on rising during the last forty years. Now much steeper rocks and overhangs are tackled which would have been left severely alone before the war. The advance has tended to be made by men of less than median height, great strength, a good power to weight ratio and very strong fingers to make the maximum use of the small holes on very steep rocks. In the early 1950s men such as Joe Brown and Don Whillans were making the running, though mainly not in the Ogwen Valley. At that time the new climbs were being achieved on Clogwyn Du'r Arddu, in the Llanberis Valley and on other low-lying cliffs. Even so, Suicide Groove on the famous Suicide Wall in Cwm Idwal was climbed first in 1948 and the pendulum swung some way back to the Ogwen Valley by the early 1960s. Such climbers as Martin Boysen, Tom Herley and Dave Alcock have added a number of most impressive routes on Suicide Wall, on the cliffs to the right of the Devil's Kitchen and on the Gribin Facet. Climbing in the Ogwen Valley is still therefore very much alive though, perhaps, it does not have the glamour of some of the more spectacular climbing on precipices by the sea or in valleys at fairly low altitude. There, the current fashion seems to be to take photographs of climbers stripped to the waist, displaying their splendid torsos in full sunshine. Most of the climbs in the Ogwen Valley are high up and there is a lot to be said for being fully dressed as well as wearing a crash helmet to prevent the head from falling rock, a practice again that has only come in since the war.

MOUNTAIN TRAINING

It is difficult to tell how far the standard of climbing has increased as a result of the large number of young people attending mountain training courses, either at Ogwen or at Plas-y-Brenin at Capel Curig or other centres. Certainly, the instructors from Plas-y-Brenin have been outstanding in the climbs they have achieved and just as important have been the various clubs with huts in the Ogwen Valley, who have trained up their own new members to achieve very high standards. Mountain training has become a major industry in and around the Ogwen Valley. On the main paths round Llyn Idwal and the routes up Tryfan and the Glyderau there are a constant succession of groups of children and young people, usually clad in orange or blue anoraks learning the elements of climbing or, at least, mountain walking. Some go off in canoes on the lakes or rivers. In Cwm Idwal the parties usually carry clipboards to note things seen on the Nature Trail, or the wisdom of their lecturer, as they form a circle round him seated on boulders.

The main Mountain School in the Valley, apart from the Admiralty training, run from Tai Newyddion, and the Scout courses at their hut on the old road, is the Ogwen Cottage Mountain School. This started originally as a private concern but was taken over in 1964 by Birmingham Education Authority who built the large extension to Ogwen Cottage in 1967. The school teaches mountain skills of all kinds, but the present head insists that the courses, lasting 12 days, are socially rather than skill oriented. The 30 children on each course, coming from a variety of schools, are volunteers and are not forced in any way. The object is self-discipline and self-appraisal. Usually, the children only like mountain walking if it it exciting. So they scramble up the North Ridge of Tryfan, Bristly Ridge and Crib Goch on the Snowdon Horseshoe. They are on the mountain from 9.30 am to 4.30 pm and, after high tea, can go to the artificial ski run at Plas-y-Brenin at Capel Curig, or do night orienteering races. One night they camp in the Gwynant valley and climb Lockwood's Chimney. The course is so arranged that children do not go on the popular routes at weekends, when they are crowded with holidaymakers.

MOUNTAIN WALKING AND RUNNING

The number of people walking and scrambling in the Ogwen Valley and on the surrounding mountain tops has been increasing steadily ever since the end of the 18th century and particularly in the last forty years. The results can be seen in the eroded footpaths, now being restored by the National Trust and the Nature Conservancy Council. The work of restoration is laborious and expensive and the bodies undertaking it tend to have different policies. The National Trust wants to open up the mountains to walkers and therefore tries to follow the best routes, which often are not rights of way. But as the land belongs to the National Trust that does not present a difficulty. The National Trust has also negotiated agreements with farmers for stiles to be erected at various points, so that walkers can be taken through farmland without causing any damage. The stiles built are solid and high enough to be seen from a distance. The Nature Conservancy Council, on the other hand, is more concerned with protecting rare plants and vegetation, hence the routing of its paths round Llyn Idwal.

It is, perhaps, surprising that a study of the map reveals that there are comparatively few rights of way in and around the Ogwen Valley. There is apparently no right of way by the miners' track from Idwal over the shoulder of the Glyderau to Pen-y-Gwryd. Nor is there any right of way along the summit of the mountains from Carnedd y Filiast, over Y Garn, the Glyderau and on to Capel Curig. There is even no right of way to Ffynnon Llugwy. Perhaps this does not matter, since, as mentioned above, most of the land is now owned by the National Trust which is in favour of access rather than against it, unlike many other landlords. A number of permissive routes have been negotiated with farmers through the UMEX scheme described later. But given the number of people wanting to walk on the mountains, it is, perhaps, surprising that there are comparatively few footpaths, whether they are rights of way or not. Nor are the footpaths way marked with coloured paint on the rocks, as in the Alps, to help the stranger find the route easily whatever the weather conditions. There has been some controversy whether the way marking of routes, as was done from the Glyderau down to Capel Curig, is the right course or not. The view of some responsible for conservation seems to be against on the grounds that it is a mistake to have too many people walking on one path, since they erode the soil. It is better that they spread out and find their own routes. Others point out that walkers seeking their own routes down the mountain are likely to damage walls by climbing over them at a number of points rather than using the stile to which the path leads.

Mountain walking is immensely pleasurable and rewarding, but it does not possess the drama of rock climbing. Walkers sometimes have to be rescued when they lose their way and are overtaken by nightfall, but the main drama of mountain rescue is that of the injured climber lying on a ledge being rescued by a skilled team of other climbers, who bring him or her down to a waiting helicopter to be whisked off to Bangor General Hospital. Sometimes a hovering helicopter, with its roter blades perilously near to the rock face, winches up an injured climber high on the North Ridge of Tryfan. For those who do not want to climb but wish to pit themselves more against the mountain than is afforded by walking, there is the challenge of fell running. The most famous walk or run — the circuit of the 14 peaks of 3,000 feet or over — began to become really interesting in the 1930s. Starting at Snowdon and taking in Crib Goch, Elidir Fawr, Y Garn, the Glyderau, Tryfan, Pen yr Oleu Wen and finishing at Foel Fras at the easterly end of the Carnedd high ridge, the route takes in all the main peaks round the Ogwen Valley. By the late 1930s the record for the route had come down to 12½ hours, which was good going over rough mountain ridges and peaks, with a total distance of nearly 30 miles and a total ascent of about 8500 feet. There could also be the difficulty of finding one's way in mist, a real hazard particularly on the Carnedd peaks. The classic account of this great walk is in Thomas Firbank's book *I Bought A Mountain* about his sheep farm at Capel Curig. Through shortening the route by plunging down a spur at Crib Goch and by other devices, Thomas Firbank managed in 1938 to get the time down to 8 hours 25 minutes, with his wife Esme taking only 1 hour longer. The Firbanks and their compansions became adept at running very fast downhill — one of them took only thirteen minutes from the top of Tryfan to the A5 at Ogwen. That, of course, is not the end of the race, since the tired competitors then have to climb the steep slopes of Pen yr Oleu Wen and find their way over the Carneddau. During the war, with fit young soldiers doing the race, the time came down below six hours. The record in 1973 was 4 hours 40 minutes. It may be less now. The most popular time for doing the walk, or run, as it has become, is on the weekend nearest mid-summer day. Then several hundred runners set off from the top of Snowdon, though perhaps only 50 or 60 complete the course.

Almost as gruelling is the Snowdon Marathon, run in October each year from Llanberis over Pen-y-Pass down the Nant Gwynant, past Beddgelert and back to Llanberis by way of Llyn Cwellyn and Waunfawr. This is a road race and does not touch the Ogwen Valley, but it is remarkable in that, given the need to climb more than 2000 feet in the course of the race, it must be the toughest marathon in the world. In 1985 the winner got round in 2 hours 28 minutes. No doubt the people who do well in the Snowdon Marathon also are adept at the fourteen 3000 feet peaks run. But most people will continue to be content with walking at a fairly leisurely pace round the Ogwen Valley mountain tops knowing that they can vary the length of the walk according to the weather by coming down into one of the numerous cwms, whichever fits their purpose.

MOUNTAIN RESCUE

Before the last war climbers, sometimes helped by shepherds and quarrymen, carried out their own mountain rescues. There was no organised service but the police had (and still has) a responsibility to search for missing persons, including climbers and walkers who had disappeared in the moutains.

In the war an RAF mountain rescue team was formed at Valley airfield on Anglesey primarily to rescue air crew who had crashed on the mountains. With intensive flying training in North Wales there were many such crashes, enough for a whole series of guide books to be brought out after the war plotting the exact site and type of aircraft. Soon after the war when metal prices were high, scrap metal merchants brought down some of the wreckage. But even today there is plenty of evidence of crashes on mountains around the valley. The shattered remains of a fighter can still be seen at about 1500 feet up on the west side of Cwm Perfedd where a stream washes fragments down lower every year. And at 2500 feet on a shoulder of Carnedd Dafydd, overlooking Ffynnon Lloer, the engine and some of the fusilage of a bomber are still to be seen.

As the numbers of climbers and walkers increased after the war it became apparent that it was not practicable to rely entirely on the RAF mountain rescue team, even though it was made much more effective by the back up of the RAF air sea rescue helicopter service. So a mountain rescue team based at Ogwen Cottage was founded in 1964 to match the team already operating on Snowdon from Pen-y-Gwryd. The Ogwen Team was to cover all the mountains round the Ogwen Valley from Capel Curig, over the Carneddau to the sea. On occasion the team have even carried out a rescue on Moel Siabod.

In 1986 the team was made up of 53 volunteers with Dr. Tony Jones, a lecturer in Oceanography at the University College of North Wales at Bangor, in charge. The team is normally called out by the police who have received a 999 call for help. When the accident is in the Ogwen Valley the team carrying out the rescue, the number depending on the complexity of the operation, are based in a small square bungalow at Bryn Poeth just to the east of Llyn Ogwen. Bryn Poeth was originally built as a keeper's cottage with good all round vision which, together with excellent wireless and telephone links, make it a good operational HQ, manned every weekend and public holiday. If there is an accident away from the Ogwen Valley the wireless equipment is such that a temporary HQ nearer the scene of the rescue can easily be set up. The rescue team itself is always in radio contact with HQ.

Sometimes the rescue team, searching for a missing person, uses dogs, Alsatians and Labradors, which rely on air, rather than on ground, scent. There are expert dog handlers in the team. On many occasions the team will request the RAF at Valley for a helicopter to pick up an injured climber or walker. The RAF, subject to getting permission from the Air Sea rescue HQ for Northern Britain at Pitreavie Castle, normally provides a helicopter very quickly. The helicopter crews are highly trained to hover when necessary just above narrow ridges or near rock faces, even when winds are gusting strongly and there is a risk of the rotor tips hitting the rocks.

In the past five years the Ogwen team has, on average, been called out 33 times a year and helped 50 people. Lamentably, every year there have been several deaths and a number of head and spinal injuries needing special equipment to get injured people off the mountains. Casualties due to exposure have been going down in recent years thanks to more climbers and walkers using really water-proof clothing and survival bags.

It is difficult to generalise about mountain accidents other than to record that their number has remained fairly constant in recent years, although the numbers of climbers and walkers on the mountains has probably increased.

As has always been the case, many accidents are due to lack of thought or failure to take the right equipment. For instance, in February 1984 the Team's report read, "A party of three wandered a little aimlessly onto and up the East Face of Tryfan. They were eventually extracted from South Gully. It was a fine night. Their equipment and experience were really not up to the ice and snow conditions". Or, in March the same year, "Due to sheer incompetence of the companion, a heavy snowfall and a late start, a middle-aged man became stranded on the summit of Tryfan. He was found uninjured and guided to safety". In February 1983, "A young man soloing on snow in Cwm Bochllwyd lost the easy way down. During his descent he tripped over his crampons and fell some 100 feet. He fractured his tibia and fibula. The strength of the wind added complications for both the Team and the helicopter. The casualty was lowered down the back wall, then winched aboard the aircraft. The helicopter had held a hover for 45 minutes in darkness while the lower was completed".

But occasionally the really experienced party of climbers needs help. In February 1984, "A well equipped and experienced party of four was avalanched out of the top of Central Gully on Ysgolion Duon. (*Black ladders* in the Llafar valley). Two were injured and two died. One of the injured walked out to summon help. In a fine display of night flying, lighted by a barrage of flares, the helicopter evacuated one of the injured. The two bodies were carried out".

Sometimes a walker is lucky when taking risks. In late November 1985 "A solo walker slipped on snow on Glyder Fach. He suffered slight head injuries. During a short break in the weather he was lifted off by C Flight 22 Sqn. He was fortunate that his shouts for help were heard by a passerby". Not only this author might well say there but for the grace of God went I.

CHAPTER 10

Conservation

Over the past 30 years strenuous efforts have been made to safeguard the beauties of the valley. Great progress was made in the 1950s when the National Trust acquired most of the valley and its surrounding mountains from the Penrhyn Estate, the Snowdonia National Park was set up and the Nature Conservancy acquired Cwm Idwal. The work of conservation has since been continued with increasing effectiveness and looks like being strengthened. But have these efforts been, to some extent, wasteful because of at least seven public and private bodies being concerned and there being some degree of duplication? In any case, are not these efforts, perhaps, doomed to ultimate failure because of the pressure that looks like growing to reduce sheep farming subsidies? The sheep farmers are, at present, the most effective managers of the landscape. If they give up, or become impoverished because the rate of subsidy is inadequate, what would happen to the valley?

On the other hand, it can be argued that the growing support for rural conservation throughout the country is becoming so powerful politically that the state will, in future, have to do more to reinforce voluntary efforts. There is already some provision for agricultural subsidies to be devoted to conservation as well as food production. This, at present, is on a small scale but could grow, particularly since it is very much in line with Common Market philosophy and, indeed, the EEC directives.

There are at least seven bodies concerned with the Ogwen Valley, three of which, the National Trust and the Nature Conservancy Council and the Countryside Commission, have countrywide responsibilities. The other four concentrate on Wales and in descending order home in more and more on the Ogwen Valley – the Council for the Protection for Rural Wales, The Snowdonia National Park Authority, the Snowdonia National Park Society and the Friends of the Dyffryn Ogwen. The Nature Conservancy Council, the Snowdonia National Park Authority and the Countryside Commission are publicly financed; the other four bodies rely on voluntary subscription, except that the National Trust gets some money from the Countryside Commission for land purchases and wardening.

THE NATIONAL TRUST

Of the seven bodies, the National Trust has the most influence in the valley as landlord of nearly all the farms and owner of most of the surrounding mountains. Its main problem is how best to allow the maximum access for the public to the mountains, without getting in the way of farmers earning their living from sheep farming. The Trust's present policy is against amalgamation of farms so as to keep as many farming families in the valley as possible.

One approach to a solution has been for the Trust to provide stiles and to rebuild eroded footpaths to help the walker, and to help the farmer by improving farm houses and barns, by repairing some of the drystone walls and by itself planting trees or providing trees for its tenants to plant.

Most of the mountain drystone walls, as opposed to those on or near the valley floor, were built at the time of the enclosures in the late 18th or 19th centuries. Hence some are straight. They were not always well built and many have been replaced with wire fences which first came in about 1860. Now the two National Trust wardens who live in the valley, with the help of the Manpower Services Commission and voluntary labour, have launched on a programme of repairing and rebuilding some of the decaying walls. On some summer days over twenty people, half of them volunteers may be at work on the walls, with the same number rebuilding footpaths and planting trees. For instance, the wall at Bwlch Tryfan has been rebuilt with good stiles where the path comes up to the wall, so the walkers can get over without dislodging stones. The new wall is of help to the farmer at Gwern-y-gof Uchaf by preventing sheep from evading the gatherers by escaping through the old gaps that used to exist in the wall and getting mixed up with the Blaen-y-nant sheep. It also provides good shelter for sheep and discourages visitors' dogs from chasing them. Some gaps in the wall along the old road in Nant Ffrancon have been filled in and now there is a four-year project to rebuild the wall which runs high up from Cwm Idwal to Cwm Coch above Pentre. The farmer welcomes the walls being repaired at the landlord's expense, and the National Trust find that, in return, farmers are more willing to fall in with the Trust's policy on tree planting and routes for walkers over farmland and on up the mountains. The National

Trust warden hopes to have all the main mountain walls and buildings on farms owned by the Trust in good shape within the next few years.

Over the last five years the Trust has also been more active in tree planting. One notable achievement is the shelter belt of alders and willows along the south side of the A5 at Gwern-y-gof Uchaf, now to be extended along the old road that runs parallel to the A5 thus forming a horseshoe shaped wood. Gwern means in Welsh the place where alders grow and Helyg, which is just down the road, means willows. So the choice of trees seems a good one.

The Trust has an extensive programme for planting oak, ash, alder and willow along the Ogwen river on Blaen-y-nant and Pentre land. The land below Tai Newyddion is also to be planted to join up with the existing wood along the river. There is to be a small copse at Ffrancon House at Tyn-y-maes and the Trust hope to be able to replace the dead hawthorn trees on the slopes above Ty Gwyn. If these plantings all flourish and are extended, it is possible that in about 50 years time Nant Ffrancon will be well wooded again. Sheep will have to be kept out of the new woods but, if the spread of bracken can be checked, perhaps by biological methods such as the South African moth which feeds on bracken shoots, the loss of pasture due to tree planting could be more than made up.

The Trust has done a lot to help walkers by providing stiles over walls and rebuilding footpaths. It is particularly keen that the rebuilt footpaths, often with stone steps and drains to take away rainwater, thus avoiding erosion, should blend into the landscape. So the Trust only uses natural materials, such as the local stone, in repairing footpaths and rejects the use of stones in wire cages which are often seen along roads to reinforce embankments. The Trust's wardens work closely with their opposite numbers in the Snowdonia Park Authority and the Nature Conservancy Council in tackling erosion on mountain paths.

In spite of a lot of good work by the Trust and the other conservation bodies, some farmers are wary of visitors because they may bring trouble in their train. A few will lose their way and knock down the top courses of the drystone walls they climb, or bring dogs which will chase pregnant ewes. Others may even sue farmers, if they are bitten by the sheepdogs, or if they hurt themselves by slipping on stiles. Farmers therefore are likely to be suspicious of mountain walkers until they get to know them. It is difficult for the farmer with no spare money to welcome walkers whose actions could conceivably cost him dear. The National Trust and the National Park Authority do their best to overcome this understandable suspicion by putting up good slip-proof stiles and by erecting notices about keeping dogs on leads, particularly at lambing time. But neither body indemnifies farmers against visitors' damage and, indeed, some walkers will still let their dogs chase sheep high up on the mountains out of sight of the farmers — a most dangerous practice.

Even grants to protect small woods by fencing, essential to the long-term survival of woodlands, are not always welcomed by farmers, since sheep can find shelter in the winter in unfenced woods.

Cwm Idwal is the best known of the seventeen nature reserves the Nature Conservancy Council possesses in Snowdonia. Cwm Idwal is remarkable not only for its striking evidence of the Ice Age but also for its rare mountain plant communities, for the work being done both to encourage these plants to grow by protecting them from grazing sheep and by checking the erosion of soil and the deadening effect of peat draining into Llyn Idwal. The setting up of the reserve in 1959 did not stop free access to Cwm Idwal where some of the best rock climbing in the valley is to be found, and through which runs the much frequented path from Idwal to the Devil's Kitchen and over to the Llanberis Valley. There is also a first rate nature trail circling the lake.

That the Cwm Idwal reserve has been a success is largely due to the work of the remarkable men who have been its wardens. The first of these, Evan Roberts, spent many years as a quarryman. When he was thrown out of work through the closure of his quarry he passed his days climbing the mountains and teaching himself to become an expert botanist with a great flair for botanical drawing. His pictures still feature prominently in major exhibitions. In time, he became blind but still lives at Capel Curig, having on retirement been awarded an honorary degree by the University College of North Wales. He was succeeded by an outstanding professional botanist based on the

Nature Conservancy Council Research Centre in Bangor.

Over the years, these wardens have done much to protect rare alpine plants, not only the famous snowdon lily *(lloydia serotina)* and the not quite so rare purple saxifrage *(saxifraga, oppositifolia)* with its striking red/pink flowers appearing in March, while snow is lying, but also to conserve the natural habitat of more ordinary plants and animals. They have shown how the more intensive sheep farming carried on since the war has tended to drain the mountain pasture of essential minerals and how it is possible to get patches of peat to regenerate. Just as important has been to stop peat washing into the lake where it would kill water plants by preventing photosynthesis as a result of a layer of peat particles forming just above the lake bottom. This is done by damming an area of peat and allowing soil to wash over and cover up the peat. Then cotton grass, heather and eventually trees, such as alder, willow and rowan, grow up.

The nature reserve is too small to enable animals such as the mountain hare to breed again in the district. The mountain hare has, for some time, only been native to Scotland. In 1890 the then Lord Penrhyn introduced a number from Scotland and their descendents — white in winter — were to be seen on the Glyderau up to about 1960. There are feral goats on Tryfan and the Glyderau and a flock of about 15 thrives at Dinas Emrys near Beddgelert. The warden can also point to small stone circles in Cwm Idwal, dating back at least to the 18th century, in which the kids of domestic goats were confined when the nannies went searching for food on the rocky ledges surrounding the cwm. The 18th century farmer knew that the nannies would return to feed their kids and hence could provide milk for the shepherd as well. There are now many more peregrine falcons around, thanks to the banning of D.D.T. and perhaps to their being able to feed on the mice breeding in the long grass which has grown in the experimental squares fenced off to keep out the sheep. Foxes abound, even though the local Fox Society, run by farmers in the valley, pays £5 for each brush. The present warden would like to see the red deer return, after an absence of about 300 years, but recognises this could not happen unless there were far fewer people on the mountains.

THE SNOWDONIA NATIONAL PARK AUTHORITY

Of crucial importance in work of conservation of the valley is the Snowdonia National Park Authority which is responsible for a huge area of mountainous land right down from Conwy in the north to Aberdyfi in the south and Bala in the east. The Park Authority, like the other nine national parks in England and Wales, is run as part of local government but with special arrangements which recognise its national importance. The Park Authority has the specific duty to protect the natural beauties of the countryside and to provide for recreation. It is financed as to 75% through funds provided by the Exchequer on the advice of the Countryside Commission, and as to 25% from Gwynedd County Council. Its members are drawn two-thirds from county and district councillors and the other one-third are nominated by the Secretary of State for Wales on the advice of the Countryside Commission. The Authority has about £1¼ million a year to spend, but could usefully spend a lot more. Its grants has, however, been rising in real terms in recent years.

The Authority's powers to prevent environmental damage in Snowdonia in general, and in the Ogwen Valley in particular, are limited. For instance, the Authority has not been able to ensure that roads built up mountain-sides by the Forestry Commission and sheep farmers fit in with the natural contours of the mountains. It failed to stop the Welsh Water Authority building a straight, ugly macadam road from the A5 to Ffynnon Llugwy in 1975. It has had powers to influence the design of agricultural buildings such as barns, but only recently have these been extended to siting and to farm and forest roads being brought under planning control.

The Authority has general planning powers for the area but its decisions on such matters as water supply, electricity generation and mining have sometimes been overruled on appeal to the Secretary of State for Wales. Moreover, it has no planning powers over agricultural activities and afforestation. It has to rely on consultative arrangements, which do not always work well, and persuasion which is not always effective. It can, however, object to the payment of agricultural grants where these would damage the environment, and now that the Welsh Agricultural Department, the Forestry Commission and the Welsh Water Authority are required by statute to pay more regard to conservation when planning new developments, or in awarding grants to farmers, the National Park Authority should carry more weight. Even so, the ordinary citizen is often surprised to find that developers can so easily encroach on the National Park.

As elsewhere in Snowdonia, the Park Authority does its best in the Ogwen Valley to check harmful developments. In the past, the Welsh Water Authority, like the Department of Agriculture, could be pretty certain of getting its way but as the recent abandonment of the Cowlyd Ceunant Scheme may have shown, perhaps, no longer, as public and politicial support for "green policies" grows.

Rather surprisingly, the National Park Authority did not oppose the selling of Tal-y-braich Farm — just over the watershed from the Upper Ogwen Valley — for forestry. In the end however it was the National Trust and the Park Society which prevented this happening by raising enough money from the public to buy the land and thus keep sheep there instead of blocks of conifers being planted. But the National Park Authority has been concerned at many other instances of the Forestry Commission or private forestry interests trying to buy land. As such interests were usually able to offer a higher price than the owner could get for selling the land as a sheep farm, the Authority often had to give way. But thanks to the pressure of public opinion they have increasingly been able to stop further excessive afforestation in Snowdonia.

The Authority has nine of its own wardens, two of whom are based on Betws-y-Coed and who are frequently in the Ogwen Valley. Their activities in the valley have supplemented the work of the National Trust and the Nature Conservancy, and have in part been carried out under a scheme — the Snowdonia Upland Management Experiment (UMEX) which was pioneered by the Countryside Commission in the 1970s. This experiment pointed to possible ways of reconciling the needs of farmers and holiday-makers and will be discussed further below. Here it suffices to record that through UMEX the Authority did much to reconstruct the footpaths and bridges above Idwal Cottage, to tidy up the car parks, to provide stiles especially on Tryfan and well designed way-marks incised into slates on walls and posts. The Authority also helped with some tree planting schemes.

THE COUNTRYSIDE COMMISSION

Many people would expect that given all the efforts of these bodies the valley would be kept in good shape, especially as yet another state financed organisation, the Countryside Commission, (which has a Committee for Wales) does its best to ensure that the policy followed by these bodies and others is on the right lines. The Commission's responsibilities are the conservation of the natural beauty of the countryside and the improvement of access to it for open air recreation. With a staff of 115 and a budget of £17½ million it carries out these responsibilities right across England and Wales. It has no executive powers but operates through the allocation of its grants and through its influence and advice as a result of the expertise it has built up on countryside issues, and from its experimental work. Indeed, its policy and technical advice carry a lot of weight, both at public inquiries on major planning issues and in the advice given to Ministers and government departments. Many, however, believe that the Commission should have greater powers to offset the much more formidable strength of the farming and land owning interests.

In Snowdonia the Commission has been active in helping the National Park Authority with major schemes such as rebuilding the main footpaths up Snowdon and replacing the dilapidated huts and railway station on the summit with a building more suitable for that magnificent site. The Commission also took part in the Upland Management Experiment (UMEX), the primary purpose of which was to find the best way of reconciling the interests of sheep farmers with those of holidaymakers. The method chosen was to bring farmers in to the work of conservation by the offer of grants and by trying to persuade them that it would be in their own interests to improve the opportunities for recreation in the area. The Countryside Commission put up 75% of the £40,000 spent on the experiment between 1975 and 1978. The Park Authority put up the rest. Normally, farmers contributed to the cost of improvements on their own land, for instance, in the repair of walls and the provision of stiles or the planting of trees. While not as successful as a similar scheme in the Lake District, the Countryside Commission was satisfied with the outcome in the Upper Ogwen Valley and the connecting valleys which continue on through Capel Curig down Dyffryn Mymbyr and Nant Gwynant. In these valleys virtually all the sheep farmers follow traditional methods of farming and most of the farms have been occupied by the same family for many years. According to independent interviews all the farmers who had work carried out on their farms under the project considered it a success. They saw it as evidence that the Park Authority was intent on taking account of their problems. This helped to change the attitude of some farmers, who before had distrusted the Park Authority as a planning authority which was seen as a threat to their independence of action. Perhaps one of the most important achievements was establishing new permissive paths, in places where existing rights of way did not give the walker the access he wanted to the mountains, being based on the needs of past agricultural and rural communities. Many of the paths on the farms in the Upper Ogwen Valley and neighbouring valleys are not rights of way, but have in the past been only tolerated by farmers and landowners. The object of the experiment was, where necessary, to create paths which would attract visitors away from old established rights of way, where they might do damage to farming. The interviews showed that although some farms have camping sites or provide bed and breakfast, about a third were antagonistic towards the recreational use of the land they farm and, indeed, only a quarter welcome visitors.

Most farmers, however, were largely unaware of the landscape conservation objectives of UMEX which is, perhaps, understandable since many considered the landscape had not greatly changed since they started farming. This is fortunately true of most of the Upper Ogwen Valley although the deduction that some make, that there is nothing to worry about, is certainly not true.

While, for the most part, all these nationwide bodies reinforce each others efforts, there must be some duplication, if only because they have their own specialised objectives. No doubt, in an ideal world it would be possible to produce a more streamlined organisation which might save some money but, perhaps, would lose in effectiveness just because it reduced the number of people (and their varying points of view) working to achieve a common end.

LOCAL VOLUNTARY SOCIETIES

THE SNOWDONIA NATIONAL PARK SOCIETY

So far as the Ogwen Valley is concerned, whatever good the national bodies have been doing — and they have achieved a lot — the local voluntary efforts of the Snowdonia National Park Society, the Council for the Protection of Rural Wales and the Friends of the Dyffryn Ogwen are crucial. The Snowdonia National Park Society has, since it was founded in 1969, been run by Esme Kirby who has farmed the southern slopes of the Glyderau from Dyffryn Mymbyr to Pen-y-Gwryd for nearly fifty years. She therefore knows the problems of the sheep farmer intimately and is well placed to see how best to reconcile the interests of conservation and the holidaymaker with those of the sheep farmer. Esme Kirby and the 2500 members of the Society make sure that no unnecessary development which could damage Snowdonia goes unchallenged. Sometimes, the Society loses. For instance, long sustained efforts to prevent a potentially ugly development at Pen-y-Gwryd have been overturned by the Secretary of State for Wales, and the Society was unable to stop the Welsh Water Authority building an unsightly road in the Anafon Valley because the work was done without any warning. However, the Society, with the National Trust, was successful in preventing Tal-y-braich Farm being sold for forestry and in ensuring that the embankment of the A5 in Nant Ffrancon was properly constructed of stone. The Society is sometimes criticised as being too English and too middle class, but to the extent that that is true it is a reflection of major social problems for which the Society can hardly be blamed.

The Council for the Protection of Rural Wales, which is concerned with the active protection of the countryside throughout Wales, has done well in having articles in Welsh as well as English in its Journal. The Friends of the Dyffryn Ogwen, with 200 members, has broad conservation aims throughout the Upper Ogwen Valley. It was formed specifically to monitor and, if necessary, oppose the Welsh Water Authority's proposed reservoir and treatment works at Ceunant, but is now turning its attention to the precise route of the Bethesda by-pass which threatens beautiful woodland. Like the CPRW the Friends of the Dyffryn Ogwen produces its reports in both Welsh and English and is most useful in providing a link between the National Trust and the local community.

THE NEXT FIFTY YEARS

It might be thought there is no need to worry about the future of the upper Ogwen Valley over the next fifty years. The green tide in favour of conservation is flowing strongly and is acquiring more political strength every year. Whichever party is in power, it cannot afford not to be seen to be keen on conservation. The voluntary societies are likely to become more, rather than less, vigilant in spotting threats to the area and in bringing pressure to bear on the government of the day. And towards the end of the fifty years the total UK population looks like falling; so there should be less pressure on the land. On the other hand, it seems inconceivable that the present level of agricultural subsidies will continue, whether they are provided through the Common Market agricultural policy or direct from Whitehall. At present, it looks as if subsidies for cereals will be reduced and milk quotas may be further cut. In that event, the main losers will be mixed farmers on fairly poor soil. But the small scale hill sheep farmer on the less favoured uplands should be less vulnerable because of the social need to maintain upland communities. Subsidies can be more readily justified on social grounds rather than for increased production which is no longer necessary. There are also many more smallholders in the mountains of Germany, France, Italy and now in the newly joined EEC countries of Spain and Portugal, than in the British uplands. Taken together, they form a powerful lobby from which the Welsh hill farmer now benefits, even though his farm is usually much bigger than theirs. Moreover, EEC countries do not yet produce all the sheep meat they consume, although they are likely to do so within a few years. The real threat would come if there were a marked surplus resulting from mixed farms on poor soil switching from milk and cereals to sheep, or even worse if the barley barons of East Anglia also switched to sheep.

If, indeed, subsidies are maintained at about the present level for the hill sheep farmer, the valley should stay broadly in its present state, though, perhaps, with a higher standard of conservation as all the good work of the conservationists over the past 25 years bears fruit. If, for example, the policies advocated in the Countryside Commission report *A Better Future For The Uplands* were adopted by the Government the outlook would, indeed, be good. Broadly, that policy is, while maintaining the present level of support to hill sheep farmers, to share it out differently in the uplands so as to encourage both food production and conservation, such as the maintenance of farm buildings and walls, and the planting of copses, shelter belts and, particularly, broad-leafed woodlands. The same policy would discourage farming operations which were damaging to the environment, such as large scale forestry in the wrong places, the building of mountain roads which took no account of natural contours and the erection of unsightly farm buildings. At the same time, the farmer would, where suitable, be encouraged to seek other sources of income such as tourism.

A step in this direction has recently been taken in the Common Market scheme for environmentally sensitive areas announced in August 1986. Six such areas, including the Cambrian mountains, but not Snowdonia, have been designated in England and Wales. Under the scheme farmers will be paid from £25 to £100 an acre to conserve the countryside rather than squeezing every last ounce of output from it. The object is to treat the countryside as a public good and farmers as its stewards. The Department of Agriculture will negotiate 5 year contracts with farmers under which payments will be made for agreed work to safeguard the local landscape and wild life. If Snowdonia is eventually included in the scheme, farmers in the valley might find a new source of funds to offset reductions in present subsidies provided they agreed to enter into a five year contract.

It seems inconceivable that subsidies would be abolished. But if, because of some major financial or political crisis in the EEC or in Britain, subsidies were withdrawn, expert opinion differs as to what would happen in the valley. Some think sheep farming would end entirely and that the mountains would, in time, be covered with scrub and coarse grass unless there were enough goats and deer brought in to keep the vegetation down. A few might even welcome the valley and, indeed, the rest of Snowdonia becoming a wilderness again. Eventually, the forests which used to cover the mountains up to a height of 1500 - 2000 feet might grow up again and polecats and pine martins might return. The ruins of deserted farms would be hidden in the tangle of undergrowth on the valley floor. But a deserted valley would be depressing to most people, who prefer the present landscape, admittedly created by sheep farmers, in which the wild grandeur of the mountains is offset by the farms and meadows strung along the valley floor.

Other people consider that even if subsidies were abolished sheep farming would continue but on a ranch standard. The whole of the valley might be one ranch on which basic sheep farming would continue. There would be a high level of losses which would result from the sheep being virtually allowed to run wild as walls and fences decayed and this would have to be accepted as the necessary price to be paid for running the whole ranch with perhaps only two shepherds. The lamb crop would still be important, although vulnerable to rustlers. Perhaps only a proportion of the flock would be dipped and shorn annually, which would, in time, lead to grave losses from disease. If, after some time, such a half wild flock ran down in numbers, the mountain could be kept free of scrub by bringing in goats and, perhaps, eventually deer.

A more likely eventuality as a surplus in sheep meat develops in a few years' time, is that subsidies would be scaled down. If the cut was not severe the most likely result would be that sheep farming would carry on, but the amalgamation of farms would speed up. If the cuts were deeper, the likelihood of even more empty farmhouses could only be offset if the Government were to devote at least some of the money now going into supporting sheep farms to other ways of helping the existing farmers, for example, by small scale forestry and grants to enable them to derive more income from the many holidaymakers who come to the valley. Of these two ways of increasing offsetting earnings, forestry in the valley would not be very attractive given the slow growth of trees at that height and exposure. Big scale forestry would, of course, defeat the ends of conservation. So, tapping the holiday market looks the most promising source of income, probably by providing more accommodation for those who want to stay in the valley but are seeking more comfort than the youth hostel or camping. And if the new scheme for environmentally sensitive areas, whereby payment would be made to farmers for conservation work, is extended to Snowdonia farmers, the outlook would be more promising.

The outlook for the Upper Ogwen Valley over the next fifty years must be uncertain but at least the present trend towards "green" policies is encouraging. If Governments continue to follow public opinion in moving towards a more enlightened view about how best to conserve the uplands, the valley will benefit. This should give heart to all those who are seeking ways of maintaining sheep farming while conserving the astonishing natural beauty of the valley, which so far has survived in spite of all the assaults perpetrated on it in the last 200 years. But there will be plenty both for the sheep farmer and the private citizen to do to keep it that way.

Glossary

MEANING IN ENGLISH OF SOME OF THE WELSH NAMES
IN AND AROUND THE NANT FFRANCON

MOUNTAINS (going round the valley anti-clockwise)

Carnedd-y-Filiast	*Cairn of the Female Greyhound*
Mynydd Perfedd	*The Centre Mountain*
Foel Goch	*The Red Hill*
Y Garn	*The Cairn*
Glyder Fawr	*Big Heap of Stones*
Glyder Fach	*Small Heap of Stones*
Y Gribin	*Ridge*
Bwlch Tryfan	*Pass of Tryfan*
Tryfan	*High Pointed Mountain*
Gallt-yr-Ogof	*Hill of the Cave*
Pen yr Oleu Wen	*Hill of the White Beacon*
Craig Braich-ty-du	*Rocky Black Ridge*
Carnedd Dafydd	*Cairn of David*
Carnedd Llywelyn	*Cairn of Llywelyn*
Foel Fras	*The Rough Hill*
Ysgolion Duon	*Black Ladders*
Mynydd Du	*Black Mountain*

FARMS (working from the lower end of the valley upwards)

Nant Ffrancon	*Valley of the Mercenary soldiers*
Penisa'r nant	*Lower end of the valley*
Dolawen	*White Meadow*
Ceunant	*Ravine*
Pengarreg	*Head of the Rock*
Tyn-y-maes	*Farm of the Meadow*
Tai Newyddion	*New Houses*
Maes Caradoc	*Meadow of Caractacus*
Ty Gwyn	*The White House*
Braich-ty-du	*The House on the Dark Ridge*
Pentre	*Village*
Blaen-y-nant	*Head of the Valley*

<u>Nant-y-Benglog</u>	*Valley of the Skulls*
Tal-y-Llyn Ogwen	*End of the Lake*
Gwern-y-gof Uchaf	*Upper Smithy in the Marsh (or place where the Alders grow)*
Gwern-y-Gof Isaf	*Lower Smithy in the Marsh (or place where the Alders grow)*
Rhyd Goch	*Red Stream*
Afon Llugwy	*Clear Water River*
Tal-y-Braich	*End of the Ridge*
Gelli	*Small Wood*

CWMS — *Valley or Hollow*

Cwm Graianog	*Gravelly Hollow*
Cwm Bual	*Wild Ox*
Cwm Coch	*Red Hollow*
Cwm Cneifion	*Shearing Hollow*
Cwm Bochlwyd	*Hoary Slope*
Cwm Llafar	*Voice (babbling stream)*
Cwm Caseg	*Mare's Hollow*

LAKES

Marchlyn Mawr	*Great Horse Lake*
Llyn Clyd	*Sheltered Lake*
Llyn y Cwn	*Lake of Dogs*
Llyn Bochlwyd	*Hoary Slope*
Llyn Idwal	*Perhaps Idwal the son of Owen Gwynedd*
Llyn Ogwen	*Rapid White Water (Ancient form Ogfanw = young pig)*
Ffynnon Lloer	*Lake of the Moon*
Ffynnon Llugwy	*Well of Clear Water*

Bibliography

GENERAL

The following are invaluable for reference:—

T.M. Bassett and B.L. Davies : *Atlas of Caernarvonshire,*
Gwynedd Rural Council 1977
A.H. Dodd : *A History of Caernarvonshire,* Denbigh 1968
Dorothy Sylvester : *A History of Gwynedd,* Phillimore 1983
Royal Commission on Ancient Monuments in Wales (R.C.A.M.)
Caernarvonshire vol. 1 H.M.S.O. 1956
Penrhyn Estate Papers (Penrhyn Ms) in Archives Library of
the University College of North Wales, Bangor.
Transactions of Caernarvonshire Historical Society (T.C.H.S.)
For individual articles see below.
Archaeologica Cambria (Arch. Camb.).
For individual articles see below.

CHAPTER 3   FROM ICE AGE TO THE ROMANS

ICE AGE

A.C. Ramsay : *The Old Glaciers of Switzerland and North Wales,*
Longmans 1860 (An excellent early explanation)
Kenneth Addison : *The Ice Age in Cwm Idwal 1986*
(A companion account of Nant Ffrancon is in preparation).
Roy Millward and Adrian Robinson : *Landscapes of North Wales,*
David and Charles 1978 (see pp82-92)
Sir Harry Godwin : *History of British Flora,* Cambridge 1975
(see p. 203)

EARLY SETTLEMENTS IN AND NEAR
THE NANT FFRANCON

William Linnard : *Welsh Woods and Forests,*   National Museum
of Wales, Cardiff 1982
F.A. Hibbert and V.R. Switsur : *New Phytologist* 1976
(pp 793-807), For radiocarbon dating of Nant Ffrancon
vegetation.

Christopher Houlder : *Wales : An Archaeological Guide* (p 58)
Faber and Faber 1974
Colin Burgess : *Age of Stonehenge,* J.M. Dent 1980
R.C.A.M. Inventory Entries Nos. 492, 493, 516, 519,
532 and 534 (See above)
T.C.H.S. (See above) 1982 p. 134
Agrarian History of England and Wales, Vol. 1 Cambridge 1981
A.H.A. Hogg : *A Guide to the Hill Forts of Britain.* Paladin 1975

Chapter 4   FROM THE ROMANS TO THE TUDORS

V.E. Nash Williams : *The Roman Frontier in Wales,* 1969
Sir Ifor Williams : *The Beginning of Welsh Poetry,* ed Rachel
Bromwich. University of Wales Press, 1972
(For derivation of the name Nant "Ffrancon", which cannot be
derived linguistically from "afranc", a beaver, as often claimed.
But there is a legend that a monster beaver once lived in Llyn
Idwal).
J.R. Jones : For James Wyatt's map of the Griffith Estate in
1352 and its early history up to 1431 see unpublished thesis
deposited in 1955 in the library of U.C.N.W., Bangor.
Penrhyn Ms : See especially Nos. 163-4 and Nos. 1599
R.C.A.M. : See no. 352, 539 and 552
H.Hughes and H.L. North : *The Old Churches of Snowdonia,*
1924
E.H. Douglas Pennant : *The Welsh Families of Penrhyn,* 1985

Chapter 5   THE CHANGING VALLEY 1500 – 1820

M. L. Ryder : *Sheep and Man,* 1983
R.C.A.M. : Nos 352 and 353
Thomas Pennant : *Tours in Wales,* editions 1784 and 1810
William Williams of Llandegai : *Observations on Snowdonia,*
1802
George Kay : *General View of the Agriculture of North Wales,*
1794
Walter Davies : *General View of the Agriculture and Domestic
Economy of North Wales,* London, 1810
Edmund Hyde Hall : *A Description of Caernarvonshire*
(1809-1811), Caernarvonshire Historical Society – Record
Series No. Two 1952

ROADS

Shirley Toulson and Fay Godwin : *The Drovers' Roads of Wales,*
1977
Frank Ward : *The Ancient Track through the Nant Ffrancon,*
Archaeol. Camb. 1939
R.T. Pritchard : Articles in T.C.H.S., 1952 and 1956
Edmund Hyde Hall : op.cit. — see maps showing roads in 1811
C.G. Harper : *The Holyhead Road,* vol. 2, 1902

Chapter 6   THE QUARRY AND THE PENRHYNS

J. Rhoose Williams : *The Quarryman's Champion,*Denbigh, 1978
R. Merfyn Jones : *The North Wales Quarrymen 1874 — 1922,*
(Chapter III), University of Wales Press, 1981
Gwenno Caffell : *The Carved Slates of Dyffryn Ogwen,*
National Museum of Wales, 1983
Jean Lindsay : *A History of the North Wales Slate Industry,*
David and Charles, 1974

Chapters 8 — 10   THE PRESENT CENTURY

For background see Kenneth Morgan's *"Rebirth of a Nation"*
1880 — 1980, Oxford, 1981

SHEEP FARMING

M. L. Ryder : *Sheep and Man,* London, 1983
Thomas Firbank : *I bought a Mountain,* Harrap, 1940

MOUNTAINEERING

H.R.C. Carr and G.A. Lister : *The Mountains of Snowdonia,*
1948
Jim Perrin : *John Menlove Edwards,* Gollancz, 1984
Geoff Milburn : *Helyg. Climbers' Club,* 1985
Trevor Jones and Geoff Milburn : *Welsh Rock,* Pic Publications,
1986
Z. Leppert : *Ogwen Climbers' Club Guide,* 1982

CONSERVATION

G. Rhys Edwards : *Snowdonia : National Park Guide,* 1982
Forestry Commission : *Gwydyr Forest in Snowdonia,* 1971
F.J. North, B. Campbell and R. Scott : *Snowdonia : the National Park of North Wales,* Collins, 1949
W.M. Condry : *The Snowdonia National Park,* Collins, 1966
Countryside Commission : *A Better Future for the Uplands,* 1984

INDEX